Britain on the Ropes

Winston Payne

DEDICATION

To all my beloved wife and friends who encouraged me over the years and who pushed me to put pen to paper. This book is dedicated them.

Winston Payne

CONTENTS

ACKNOWLEDGMENTS

I wish to personally thank all of my family, friends and business associates for their contributions and inspiration. It was with their support, that I had the courage to create this book.

My exposure in the boxing world and my father's continued support when I was a young, gave me what I needed to survive and thrive in this ever changing world. I'd like to acknowledge his support and that of the boxing world. Without the family I have, the friends I have met down the years, I wouldn't have become the man I am today.

1 FÉTED AND REVERED

I came to Britain; but to Britain, I was just another immigrant off the Banana Boat. Well, the boat I boarded at St Lucia had indeed taken on board bananas. It took on lots of things, people included. It had already picked up goods and passengers from other islands in the Caribbean and was now headed for Montserrat before it would set its course eastward over the Atlantic.

I said goodbye to my father and watched him standing on the quay side as my ship sailed out into the Caribbean Sea. I remember wishing that I could have signalled to him using the semaphore code he taught me. He'd been a signaller during the war, communicating with warships coming into the harbour. But now he was frail. Brought down by an illness that had reduced the one time heavyweight boxer to a mere mortal being. And I had to earn money to support the family now.

My Atlantic Crossing ended ten days later at the Strait of Gibraltar. Our first European port of call was the Rock itself. Then we sailed on to Naples; followed by Cannes, and finally Genoa. Here I left the ship and, with other immigrants, boarded the train that would take me over the Italian boarder and across France to pick up the ferry at Boulogne. My British passport got me through customs at Folkestone and the boat train brought me to Victoria station. Then, at last I was in the welcoming arms of my mother.

My mother had settled in London, having taken up the invitation from Britain in the mid-50's for skilled workers to make up the short-fall in their labour market. As we made our way to her rented room through the grim streets of London I felt pleased that my father had stayed behind. His view of Britain, as that wonderful island to be féted and revered and who would

1

pronounce the name, "Great Britain" with honey smooth affection, would remain forever untarnished in his mind.

Well, I went straight into work. Jobs were easy to find back in 1961 - if you weren't too fussy. It was a low-paid job in a saw-mill. I stuck it for six months. Yet it had given me an idea. I'd learnt about different types of timber. I was on my way, only I didn't know it then.

I still did a lot of sports at that time. Originally I did judo but this was not my preferred sport. I went into boxing and also wrestling. I'd always been interested in boxing and used to read the exploits of the likes of James J. Corbett, Bob Fitzsimmons, Tommy Burns and Jack Dempsey. These were all strategic fighters. I got to learn that a lot of fighters developed their styles depending on their physical make-up. That was: whether to be a boxer-fighter; a logger-head fighter; or a close-in fighter.

At the time I was working in the Royal Docks, unloading cargo ships; but then they brought in containers and the work went to Tilbury. So I got a job with Berk Spencer Acids Ltd. This was in their experimental plant where they were developing new types of paint. They did this by crushing different types of material by blasting with steam. This was very interesting, but not as much as boxing was. I was growing very fast and developing in size and locally I could not get a proper heavyweight opponent in my area. They were all Light-Heavyweight - too light to spar with. I was already over 210 lbs at 20 years of age; that's a small Heavyweight.

By the time I was 21 years old I was a full-blown Heavyweight. I was very quick but I never used a high guard - the trainers didn't like that. The trainers were hard on me but I was struggling to fight my own corner; I needed to earn enough to support myself and also to send money home. To make ends meet, I'd applied to work in Berk Spencer's foundry where they did their smelting. At first they were reluctant because of my age - I was now twenty-four, and they thought that too young. They tried to put me off. But eventually I got a trial which ended up lasting seven years. The heat in the foundry was incredible. We'd get two pints of milk a day, plus a little salt to make up for what we were losing in sweat.

But the work took its toll. I couldn't quite make the grade in boxing; so, reluctantly, I threw in the towel. But I still retained my interest in it and later I found that the time I'd spent reading about fighters was to stand me in good stead. At the same time I also handed in my notice at the foundry. The management were dumbfounded. I was asked to attend a meeting. I was a little apprehensive, so I brought my union representative along with me. We entered the Board Room. There were six of them there; directors; managers; supervisors - they tried to get me to stay. They offered to send me to college, at their expense, to study metallurgy. But I declined; I thought to myself, this work is too specialised I'd never find another job in this field locally.

But I wanted to learn a trade so I joined a government training centre. There I learnt about workshop practices and precision engineering. That got me a job with Industrial Bindings in Islington who, at the time, were making parts for Blue Streak - the planned missile for Britain's independent nuclear deterrent. From there I went on to work for Petters Engineering in Middlesex.

And all the time I clung to my love of learning. I started going to evening classes. I was forever wanting to improve. I studied maths; geography; history, whatever - I lapped up knowledge avidly. Then, in 1982, I went for a job interview to work with young people who were just about to come out of school for the summer. The plan was to take them on a trip round Europe. Well, I was one of four selected out of thirty five applicants. I was the only black person to have applied. Anyway, when I went for the interview I thought there would be three or four interviewers; but when I went in I was surprised to find seven people sitting there ready to fire questions at me. They took it in turns to question me but, after the first three had grilled me, the chairman announced that I'd answered all that they could possibly want to know.

Still, I got the job. I was to be one of six leaders that were to take a group of twenty-four youngsters across the continent on a double-decker bus lent to the government by the army. So, when the time came, we crossed the channel to Calais, then drove the bus through Dunkirk to the city of Lille. Here we hit a snag. Some of the young people did not have visas - which were needed then in the days before the European Union was set up - and we could not enter Belgium. However we met a Frenchman in a café who directed us to an unmanned checkpoint and so we were able to carry on.

We drove through Belgium, Holland and northern Germany to Jutland, stopping at pre-arranged locations along the way. At Jutland, we found that nothing had been arranged. This did not deter our Danish hosts who gladly found families to look after us. From Jutland we took the ferry to Zealand and stayed a few days in Copenhagen before driving back.

Well after that I continued working as a Field Officer. My role was to meet people both inside and outside London. I was one of four. We would exchange ideas, it was very refreshing. But then Margret Thatcher closed the youth clubs so the work finished. It was then that I started working on building sites I carried on with my evening classes, but now I applied myself to obtaining City & Guilds certificates relating to the construction industry.

Not that my employer gave me any time off to study or help towards the cost. In fact, when they found out, they sacked me. I think they were worried that my desire to become multi-skilled was so that I could branch out on my own. Well that hadn't occurred to me - but now I had no choice. At first I went self-employed; but later I started my own business, 2 Pitons. The extra work though meant I had to give up the youth work; but not my studies.

It was while attending college that I first noticed how different groups approached studying. Those from India, for instance, are very studious - both male and female students - but African-Caribbeans are too casual in their approach; treating college more of a social event. Some were OK, but to many it was more "Boy meets Girl". They were much more interested in music and whilst this is good to a degree I think that overall it had a negative impact on them.

Another thing that I have noticed about African-Caribbean young people in this country is how much they are into sports; even the children. I see them as I travel by school playgrounds; it's the black kids that are always indulging in sports. Now, I have always been very keen on sports myself; but it seems to me that there is an imbalance. I have never taken too kindly to seeing too many black kids in sports and I will explain why.

I find very often that sport is often seen as their strongest point. So they are encouraged to do well at this, at the expense of neglecting other strengths. Therefore, even if they have potential or talents in other areas these were not being made the maximum use of for further advancement. Black kids are seen as talented in music - you've seen them; all good singers, singing round the same microphone. So during break-times at school they would be singing and listening to music rather than reflecting on the lessons that they had just taken. So what they had just learned vanished from their minds before it could be assimilated.

Now while I was still gaining the skills in the building trade, I did some free-lance security work at various colleges. This allowed me to see African-Caribbean students in full-time higher education. But as I watched them moving between classes I was dismayed that even here they would get together to listen to music. So once again they were not digesting what they had just been taught by their tutor. And here, I believe, is where the seeds are sown for producing the stereotyped image of young African-Caribbean's. Because, with all this emphasis on sport and music, it's no wonder that so many go down that route. Not that this in itself is such a bad thing - they certainly gain a sense of self-worth and affirmation; yet there are only so many opportunities to succeed in these fields. Therefore a lot of them end up in limbo. Add to this the close proximity to each other where they live and you can see that their parents are powerless to get their children to alter course. Especially when, clustered together like this in neighbourhoods where everyone shares the same mindset, they become resentful of the System that - having lured them into taking easy options - now blames them for underachieving.

Yet a lot of Caribbean parents, and I am Caribbean myself, feel that there should be a new emphasis: that of discipline and diplomacy, coupled with a measure of psychology. I'm not suggesting that psychology should be studied as a subject - although if this opens up avenues not previously considered; then all to the good. No, what I have in mind is the sort of psychology that would enable our young people to gain an insight into image. Image is important. It tells you how to conduct yourself; how to be presentable, and it reflects the way you portray yourself to others. This should be part of education.

But right now, if you look at pop groups and singers on television, they mostly give an image of 'hard boiled'. Few present themselves with a sophisticated image. Our younger ones are latching on to this. Yet it should not be all brawn and no brain or all talent and no sophistication. No; rather discipline, honesty and proper ideology - that is what holds the world together. Not necessarily new ideas; new ideas still have to have proper substance. Without any substance they are meaningless.

So what happens when our youngsters grow up and they find that they have to present themselves to someone? Chances are they won't make a good impression. More likely they'll be brooding; as though they're not expected to be civil. They've got to have that in-built self-confidence. It should permeate through their features. They should understand how important the manner in which they approach someone is. Teaching them how to shake hands; how to be welcoming. This should be what schooling is all about.

The education system should help by encouraging young people from a very early age to learn about the lives of people in the past. People like Nelson Mandela because, when he came out of prison - having been incarcerated for so long - he talked only of reconciliation, not revenge. Therefore this will teach them discipline; it will encourage them to aspire to a sound work ethic, to have wonderful presentation and the ability to walk away from trouble.

Such training would serve them immensely well; far better than a formal education could.

Sometimes, I feel, we try to educate them in too many subjects. It's like the schools are obsessed with GCSE results. But, even if good exam grades were to equip them in furthering their careers, is it doing them that much good? Obviously they are going to have to earn a living, but that 'dash-for-cash' can be overwhelming for some of them.

2 CAUGHT BY A SUCKER PUNCH

Now this view of Britain is not just about African-Caribbean youth. It is also about what I see as the visible manifestations of British politicians' ideology. That is; an occurrence presented to the British public which supposedly is a modern day phenomenon of progressive existence yet in reality draws parallel to a pugilist ducking between the ropes. Our politicians, it seems to me, are far too eager to welcome all comers with no difference, while proclaiming themselves to be the custodians of the public interest.

But was it a lack of foresight or the compulsion of ideology that railroaded the British public into a one way trip to eternal oblivion? Because frequently we are told migration is good for this country. This has, however, become a sad irony and all those who have been in support of the EU concept in its current form should be placed on trial by a People's Tribunal. Therefore, promises made by those who aspired to high office, during the lead up to the 2010 General Election should now act appropriately and make good their promises of "Power to the People".

Myself, as a migrant who has made this beautiful country my home, I can see that with a land size less than a hundred-thousand square miles it gives the British people a hundred thousand reasons to say to the spineless politicians, "We have long passed saturation point." I see these politicians as Muppets; so blinkered within their ideology that they keep blabbing about capping Non-EU immigration. In retrospect, the cap is drawn too far down - obstructing their line of vision; thus preventing them from seeing the waves of migrants wreaking havoc to the aspirations of Small British Businesses and the Construction Industry.

This is because people from EU countries - who have existed on predominantly lower wages - are quite prepared to enter the UK Jobs' Market at half the rate of their UK counterparts. Is there any British politician sufficiently insane to suggest we should compete on a downward trajectory? Yet so endemic is the trail of devastation inflicted by the creation of savage price cutting that those who pursue this form of economic navigation leave no margin for taxation. It is a matter of rapid "kill and grab". The so-called EU partners in the main are, and will remain, much more nationalistic than those from Commonwealth countries where the Union Jack has created an indelible print. In fact, in lots of these territories they view Britain as a close family relation.

No, the damage is being inflicted by those from mainland Europe. We see the humiliating spectacle of Britain; reeling on the ropes - its defence in tatters - being pounded at close quarters by body-shots from neighbours who often, and repeatedly, punch below the belt. Uncontrolled immigration, irrespective of where from, is tantamount to legalised criminality. Yet Britain is seen by many as a country with a highly sensitive underbelly built on the construct of a digestive biscuit. Soaking it above and below the belt as it's crumbling, while their European partners mercilessly continue to dish out their brand of wet leather.

So, with the British people in terms of military might no longer great; and who, like chewing-gum, are being stretched to meet the ever ongoing demands placed upon them, it is no wonder that they are now stumbling and weakening in the middle. No doubt this is the reason why we are so attractive to the outside world. It would be far better giving priority to the Home Front and be financially obese in the middle. Then we will be able to fulfil our personal objectives. Yet we are literally at full stretch - I REPEAT, full stretch - simply trying to cope with our infrastructure. Housing, for example, is a nightmare and unless population growth can be curtailed I fear this nightmare will bring us to the next chapter where the dustbin will be the home of the impoverished ones. I can even see future generations scouring the pages of history and looking back at the early part of the twenty-first century yet, despite all its trials and tribulations, still being envious of us.

In ring warfare, with two opponents in combat, one would be described as being caught by a sucker punch. And those punches are delivered by our neighbours below the belt; draining the energy out of the British system because for many years we had Border Control but now, for most of Europe, we have an Open Door policy towards them. Therefore optimism is now a precious requirement and reality will call for a critical analysis of its concepts, but the limits of human knowledge may impose restrictions. From an external position we may be able to distinguish cause and effect and it would be fascinating to see the parallel of such doctrines which advocate the free flow of movement.

Could, I wonder, it be demonstrated to have been successful - even as a pilot scheme? Any answer, between positive or negative, must surely show this to be the abject failure of a short sighted doctrine. Of course some people will, from time to time, come face to face with racism or prejudice. This lovable country has, like all others, a variety of characters. That has to be expected. Every corner of the globe has its own permutation. Britain has a beauty of welcome and tolerance almost unrivalled let alone surpassed. The British people require leaders of authentic pedigree to do justice to the people.

So what, I repeat, is the advantage of being in Europe? Is the government trying to say that migration is good for the country? Where is their evidence? Did our politicians know the consequences of 'Open Borders' when they plunged us into this so-called union? Or was this just a line they sold us; and we went along with it. However, these sorts of decisions have a profound impact on our society which is why I have used the analogy of a boxing match to describe it.

As I mentioned earlier, I had read a lot about boxing during my childhood in St. Lucia.

My father had encouraged me to read. In fact, that's putting it mildly. You see, I was eight when my father became ill. Without his income, my mother was forced to take a job in Britain and send money back. So my father needed me at home which meant that I could no longer go to school. However, my father had been a school teacher so he was able to tutor me at home. And not only that, but he let me join the local library where I read everything I could lay my hands on; especially magazines from Britain. My dad loved the British. You couldn't say nothing against Britain. At the library I would read The Illustrated London News. Later I read the New York Times and Newsweek. Then the Christian Science Monitor which was regarded at that time as one of the best newspapers in the world. I read many local papers as well; such as the Barbados Advocate, Trinidad Guardian and the Jamaica Daily Gleaner - now they have what they call the Jamaica Weekly Gleaner.

But learning mathematics was not so good. My father would test me every Saturday. If I did well, he'd let me go swimming Sunday mornings. If not -

it was chores instead. So I learned well. And I am glad I did now because having a business to run means that maths is essential. Not that I needed to know much maths when I first started work. Then I was more interested in boxing.

Back then I used to spar with a heavy-weight boxer and I gave him ideas on boxing. He was a professional and he rose to Number 4 in the Heavy-weight league. One of his trainers was Frank Blank who also trained with Terry Lawless who went on to manage Frank Bruno and Johnny Stracy who was a champion in the '7O's. There was also Ralph Charles, Peter Bodington and Johnny Gardener. Johnny Gardener used to live in Hackney and because I was always reading about the strategies of boxing I was able to pass this information on to him. No one knew who I was. They would see me there, in the gym, when they were talking about boxing. They would mention a name from the past and I would be able to talk about that person.

However, back in the '70's there was one boxer - George Dulaire - who tried to persuade me to obtain a trainers' license. Unfortunately I didn't have the money or the back-up to make a serious effort. Still, I was happy to do it for fun because I enjoyed it. If I was able to be of assistance I would help. Anyway George always asked me to come with him, not that I was allowed to coach him but sometimes, in training, I would whisper things to him; things about his opponent that I had read. I could, for instance, tell him that his opponent would fight in a particular way.

Sometimes we would go to Solihull where they had the Anglo-American Sports club, which was a Members Only club. No one was allowed to shout there. Then there was a place in Bedfordshire. I used to like moving about. It was great, very fascinating.

So you can see how important reading is; and how it can be such a useful skill to have - especially when you talk to people. It really helps with your communication skills. I kept in with the boxing scene for quite a while. Once I was helping Tony Villanor, who I introduced to boxing at the Black Lion club, and I spotted Terry Spinks' boxing gloves hanging on the wall. These were the ones he used when he won the Fly-weight Olympic Gold Medal at Melbourne in 1956. That was another thing that I remembered reading about when I was a boy.

Now, I know a lot of parents take their children to sporting events and this is all very well. But some of those sports then become very much a religion. Everything, just like the medication we take, should have a balance. It's like walking a tight-rope; you need to keep good balance. So, irrespective of whatever we are doing, we should not be too overbalanced on one side. It's the same with reading newspapers. As I said, I would read the newspapers as a kid; and I read a lot about boxers and their fights. But I kept a balance. I also read other news items such as criminal cases and spies - people like Maclean and Burgess; the ones in the Foreign Office. Then I started reading about politics; what the British and American administrations were doing; especially in the Caribbean region. I never thought of the world as a dull place, and because of this I now enjoy meeting people. But if kids just buy a paper for the football they're not seeing what's going on in the world at large. There is a down side to all this. Because if you take a lot of the youngsters and there is something of national concern that is of great prominence and you ask them about it they'll probably ask you, "What are you talking about?" But if you ask them the score of the previous night's match they can tell you even if it wasn't their team that was playing.

You see, when these young people look in the paper, they go straight to the sports pages.

They might look at the headlines, but by the time they get to Page-3 they have forgotten the argument. Now this imbalance; we have it nation-wide. It is not just the black kids it's everywhere. There are still a lot of places where they have youth centres and these are good as it gets the kids off the street. All the same I find that the emphasis should be more than just sport. Out on the street they are just meeting like-minded friends, and once in the youth centres it's the same. All they do in these centres is more sport. Therefore their brains are not developing and they are not getting 'battle-hardened'. This means that they are unable to meet the demands and the challenges that in reality they are likely to encounter.

Now in many sports, to be a champion; to be at the top of your game, you have to go through the Pain Barrier. That is necessary to become a true champion. And there are many instances in real life - apart from sport - that when it comes to earning a livelihood, you've got to be prepared to go through the Pain Barrier. You can't simply surrender in abject failure, dropping hands aside, saying, 'This is too hard' or 'I'm not going for it'. Whether it is sunshine, whether it is snow or a cold day because you know it is not going to be like this for ever. So the time you have to spend when it's like this; then you do it. I did it as a brick-layer. Cold days; a black man: the back of my hands - black; but the palms of my hands white. White and tender. I am in the freezing drizzle laying bricks at the top of the scaffold. But I saw the day through and when I got home I'm glad to be home. But I have the Iron Will the next morning to be out there to earn a living, and I never fled from it.

3 THE KAMIKAZE HIGHWAY

Now this view of Britain reeling on the ropes should not mislead you into thinking that I am knocking this wonderful island. For it is the very affection that I hold for Great Britain and its people that is the reason for my distress. It is the political slough of despondency into which we have fallen that brings me to put pen to paper. I have never ceased to be amazed by the high level of tolerance exemplified by the British people. Their patience and perseverance is surely beyond the call of duty. I will not subscribe to people who are in, or aspire to, positions of representation going around faking facial expressions of authenticity.

How happy are we when the issue of Europe arises? Are we, in very simple words, thinking, it's an advantage to be in Europe? Like, "Migration is good for the country," or something? The government govern for the entire country. Whenever two sides of the equation are available, one on its own is insufficient as evidence. We want the "Pro's" and "Cons". Evidence is the bottom line here.

Yet we seem to be in a constant battle between Ideology; Necessity, and Reason. The ideology, being primarily guesswork, can hardly provide an explanation when it has not been tested; let alone found to conform to facts. Although, as a viewer of knowledgeable television, I have witnessed some questions that were asked yet were answered as, "They come here we go there".

In so doing one should question the validity of such concepts and ask whether they are the ultimate characteristics of reality. For there is a need to demonstrate, unambiguously, a definition to a particular conclusion within the institutions whose command we are to follow. Is there a set of doctrines to which we are all requested to comply as a benchmark of civility? If so, will they ensure impeccable understanding?

When tough issues are presented, by perfectly valid questions being asked, why then do politicians fall into epitomising a defensive posture? This is simply recycling the badly worn out track. You've heard them say. "I do not intend .... " rather than give a definite, "Yes/No" answer. This is typical of politicians who love to sit on the fence and it inadvertently creates double sides without edges. Yet we know that later on they will say, "I said, 'I did not intend'" meaning that they had not intended to do something, but insisting that, that did not imply that they were not going to do it. Well this just re-enforces deep suspicion and broadens cynicism with everything that they espouse.

Having preached and promised to the electorate, the people and the nation with evangelical zeal, you may think that these politicians are now speaking the Gospel Truth. And not just in words; their facial expressions and body language give the impression that you could, 'Bet your life on it' their words being purer than pure. Yet the microscope, which is predominantly used for close-up objects too small for the naked eye, reveals that these politicians are just pretending. They are, in all honesty, simply trying to sell you on their line of "perceived" thinking.

Whilst to peer at such heavenly bodies, as these politicians would have you to believe they are, sets in motion the chain of reaction to acquiesce and give a semblance of credibility. However, seen in broad daylight, even without the microscope, they are not deemed to be heavenly bodies by those being invited to make such observations. My venture, probably piquant in nature, is to find truth in news; honesty in opinion and freshness in revelation; because the electorate venture to the ballot box to elect those who aspire to the political arena to be credible public servants.

On close examination, however, it seems that impulse is the main objective to implement their doctrines. There is gross failure on their part to understand the significance with which their ideals play towards the detriment of human life. Analysing these ideals shows that these public servants will swage a hammer of human economic brutality; leaving us peering into the gloom of an ocean of future misery. The British people find themselves spectators of a charade that is engulfing the nation.

Now we British are sometimes told that we should compete, because we have been having migration for over one hundred years. Yet this begs the question, 'Do the politicians understand the laws of the jungle?' Marketing

Strategy is hugely important in today's world. I remind the reader my reference of business applies to the private sector. When the demands for skilled labour is on the decline, with unimpeded flow of migrants pouring in at will, the citizens of the country are devoid of bargaining power. Reduced job opportunities ensue as a direct consequence of what is not a trickle but an endless inward flow.

The result, of blindly following such ideals and ideology, is an uncontrollable flow of people from over two dozen countries in Europe. No wonder that skilled people - now ex-workers, whose craft has been honed over a number of years - are left to rue in the dark passages of memory where previously the lights shone brightly.

Britain is effectively on a kamikaze highway while the people of this country seek from the leaders the last rites and are taken for a ride. Should their aspirations cause them to become conscious of values, then they might be critical of such ideas and skeptical of the wisdom that expounds leading an exemplary life. Would they not then, through commitment and true grit with absolute dedication to achieve success and happiness, pass such illumination of character - which is a model of example - to succeeding generations?

It is a tragic irony to see such a country as Britain - where its hard working people deserve nothing less than the best people to lead them - which once had great work ethics, knowledge, warmth, generosity and tolerance now spawning politicians who use methods of language that seek to deceive the electorate. The erosion of credible opposition is evident in their cynical comments and ambiguous replies. On all too numerous occasions where questions were asked such as, "Where are the cuts going to come from?" in the months and weeks leading up to the 2010 general election, a ready source of reply was the answer. Yet they would categorically, repeatedly, make announcements that within fifty days there would be an emergency budget should they assume office.

Within that time frame the areas of cuts were to be identified and the figures delivered.

When certain areas were specified the reply would always be, "I have no intention ..." The electorate witnessed politicians going into marathon sessions of cloak and dagger before becoming actors who displayed cynicism and set toxic examples by organising chaos and creating confusion especially when they rattled away about student fees. In partial fairness, to my limited knowledge, no promise was ever made to reduce the student debt burden. But examine the sincerity of the contrast in vociferous condemnation prior to gaining power. Language such as "Saddling students with debts" pretending to be passionate and concerned yet the ranting and raving came to an abrupt cessation. If anything, there have since been systems and methods introduced to increase the Debt Burden.

Shedding light on such misdemeanor's may well induce a change of pattern in behavior.

Clichés are banded about such as, "New kind of politics ..., " seriously; what do these words imply? Do they mean better results or greater prosperity to the nation, or are they - at best - simply hollow words that, on analysis, have no credibility?

The shifting sands of time have seen Britain no longer a part of the Big Four. This wind of change has provided us with the unenviable opportunity to witness its decline to a minor role with daily erosion of the standing it once had as a great super-power. The reason for this is, in part, the government's failure to alter our education system to meet such a changing world. They simply tinker here and there; calling some schools, "Academies," then changing their minds. But really, most of our children could benefit by being grounded in just a few core subjects. Most of what is taught in schools will never be needed. If it is - later on - then those who desire to better themselves can go to part-time colleges. In fact, part-time colleges - such as those for Adult Education - are excellent ways for learning vocational skills such as; painting and decorating, how to tile properly, knowing how to be a handyman and so forth. These skills are desirable in our changing world because, unless you belong to the upper echelons of society, you should be constantly seeking new skills and knowledge, within the limits of your available spare time.

So really and truly you don't need to go to university; unless you are going to study specific subjects in more depth. But getting so many GCSEs at school is pointless, because by the time you start work you have forgotten most of what you'd learned to pass those exams. Although, having said that, we should include foreign languages in the list of core subjects taught at school.

But I do think the kids in this country are wrapped up too much in cotton wool. There are many things that we do, if not intentionally, but they do impact negatively on the other strands of living. In the last few years we have introduced free buses for children. Now the kids won't walk two bus stops. This leads to obesity because they are becoming inactive. This inactivity does not prepare them for the harsh world. If our kids could see the sort of conditions in third world countries this might get them thinking.

The authorities should also encourage children to read more. Not "Story books" as such, but books about real events. These events would then gradually take root in their minds and within a short period of time start cultivating their attitude to life. Then, as they move into maturity, they will find not only that their attitude keeps them in good stead, but it will reap a harvest of knowledge as a result. And because of this they will be able to communicate and understand others so much more. Such abilities are of immense value.

Nowhere, right now, are these abilities more needed than in African-Caribbean children.

For these children, there is no doubt that nothing short of an educational revolution is needed because many avenues, for the majority of them, are closed. Undoubtedly there are some bright and brilliant spots, but to the bulk of the African-Caribbean population, far too many are not coming up to scratch.

The revolution which I am referring to may be debatable, but it ought to be talked about in serious manner. Certain doctrines should be taught to our children with people in the educational establishment allowed to introduce others. Those ideals that I could name are embodied in the life and times of Mahatma Gandhi and Jomo Kenyatta, both renowned leaders with vision and initiative who were international public figures of the highest calibre. And there are others who have inspired us to stand against segregation and discrimination - and to triumph against seemingly impossible odds - such as Martin Luther King; Nelson Mandela; Desmond Tutu and, from earlier time, Alexander Bustamante of Jamaica.

Transcripts of the lives and times of these people would be awe inspiring.

They would sow within the minds of children that the world does not owe anyone a living. They would teach them that you can sometimes in life be cultivated in the art of disciple, enterprise, resilience, courage and especially into the art of hard graft. That is - you have to work for it!

4 DEMOCRACY AND TABOOS

So, what have we discovered: well, that African-Caribbean young people are being stereotyped in ways that portray them as being good only in music and sport; that they have a 'hard boiled' mind-set because of the relatively closed communities in which they live, and that they appear to lack the desire to excel. As with all stereotypes, this is not a true picture; but it tends to be reinforced by sensation seeking media reports. You only have to think back to the coverage of the "disturbances" of August 2011 to know what I am talking about.

Yet, worse than this, it undermines the immense potential which these young people have. And this is why it is so vital that we continue to support them during their early years as they interact with each other via the sporting arena. But, after that, we must not abandon them. We must also make a long term investment in them as people. Then we shall be fashioning a consensus that should minimise the development of waywardness and create a more wholesome attitude; both for their own selves, and towards others. Furthermore, nurturing a sense of value and developing a profound measure of integrity avoids the creation of selfishness and, by all accounts, extends the precious gift of courtesy with the freshness of due respect to others.

Therefore, intellectuals should be appointed to implement, administrate and monitor classes. Then other individuals should be used to chronicle, in great detail, their aptitude to the brand of cultivation with their display of youthful exuberance which can be indicative of their environment and background. And then, by capturing them as a sporting group - where there is a tendency to demonstrate behaviour similar to spiny lobsters on the seabed, who follow each other - you can achieve better results by indoctrinating the leader. In this way you are getting them to strive for a higher strand of fulfilment. So, through attaining such fulfilment, this will impact with great credit onto the community and also will less adversely affect society.

However, selecting excessively high calibre individuals for such assignments could be fraught with error. Dexterity of minor adjustments should be the requirement; contrary to that may result in a flawed genius. This means that reliance on cash alone is not going to be an ideal criteria, not that anything could ever be totally satisfactory. Yet it is important that we strike a delicate blend of emotion and discipline, and identify at first hand some of these characteristics. There are many factions of society. It's not enough to simply put in more and more money and hope this solves the problem.

All the same, it makes a welcome change to see the Mayor of London Mr. Boris Johnson designate a sum of £1.3M to obtain the services of 1700 volunteers in supporting young black boys with their homework and sports activities. This should be applauded very warmly by all concerned including those in the African-Caribbean community who are regarded as their leaders. It should also be welcomed by those on the periphery of politics as well as everyone who aspires to the well-being and development of the African-Caribbean people in Britain.

In the same breath, I join with the rest and hope that many of the rest join with my way of thinking. This is a wonderful gift. It is sure to elevate the existing black community both now and in the future. We should not though run away with the idea that this is what they need to get all of the time. It should be a springboard for us to get more vociferous in telling our young men that they all have to be proactive, more enterprising and, if they don't like the situation they are in, it is not all down to the state or the government.

I daresay there are plenty of opportunities in this land to which, if our young people made a commitment and dedicated themselves, they could advance beyond their present boundaries. Tough as it may be in this country, it is still less tough than what many of their counterparts experience in foreign lands. They have great opportunities here to do more worthwhile projects, which will stand them in good stead. The more mature African-Caribbean people in the United Kingdom should not be too sentimental and needlessly patronizing in giving them any succour in believing that the world owes them a living all of the time and everything should be given to them on a plate.

Now that the government has given them the carrot, it should also give what else goes with it. For it should be known, "With the sweat of thy brow, thou shalt eat bread."

Commitment; tenacity; diligence, should be very much evident in their vocabulary. Forget about the knives and the guns and the weapons, for these are the hobbies of cowards. By going down that evil road they have, as we have seen, been stereotyping themselves right down to the lowest rung of the upright ladder.

Yet if they relish this accolade, of being at the bottom of the pile, it would greatly indicate they are devoid of dignity and they have no pride. You've got to elevate yourself from the bottom and join the train of civilisation. Stop and look objectively and look at your actions. You do not require role models only from within your own community; you should be prepared to embrace role models from any walk of life irrespective of race; irrespective of creed. A lot of the youngsters in Britain seem to believe they know it all. They have placed themselves in limbo by simply believing that they are knowledgeable; rebelling again the teachers of classes and also not particularly willing to listen to their elders either.

Consequently, when attitudes have shifted away from one and still not wisely equipped to make a safe jump to the other, they are not even in No Man's Land - they are just riding on the wind; no specific objective; too laid back for good measure. However, people do need to have educated minds. But there's not one single item that on its own would be sufficient. It's a variety of approaches; such as first identifying a person's character. Then develop splinter groups so as to allow self expression. Those who you've identified as natural leaders would become role models for the others to follow. And in this way, dealing with such problems as getting people's mind-sets to become more disciplined; because we should all be respectful. In a democracy we sometimes lose these things. Things like discipline and respect. The kids over here are too wrapped up in cotton wool. I am glad that I was brought up in the Caribbean.

So we need to talk to young people like you're one of them. This can be done by having small groups of seven or eight youngsters. Allowing them to speak, facilitating discussions and making them feel at home. Hence your consummate skill comes into play within the process of assisting the progressive development; be it social, vocational, sporting, intellect or self-confidence, any of the paths chosen, singular or multiple, makes a telling contribution to the field of humanity. Then once you have won over a few; these can then go out and engage with others. So, slowly - over time - there will be a change of mind-set throughout the youth in our society. But you're just breaking it down, bit by bit.

And the time to start is from birth; really! We are talking serious stuff. It is imperative that as soon as children are able to distinguish the differences between objects that they identify human features and creatures. In this way they quickly develop the powers of imagination and the excitement of new discovery. Environmental background may assist to determine which methods and subjects are most beneficial to apply. Illustrating a voluntary willingness to indulge in reading from an early stage is a joyful observation; for it renders immense assistance to exploring the hitherto unknown traffic of existence. Such fascination to the initial stages of learning reaps untold reward, minimises the seeds of boredom and contributes greatly to an enterprising mind.

Yet all this risks being lost even in their earliest days at school. Why? Well, we have heard quite many a topic on school class sizes which we are discovering to be growing rather than declining. Why is the system not able to achieve what - on paper - would appear to be a simple task to reverse? Well, not when the new administration of 2010 embarked on the stoppage of the school building programme. So, unless that programme is renewed - as this particular administration claims it will be - there will soon be a chronic shortage of school places. Therefore, unless something monumental comes into existence - to redress this - the problems with our young people will be exacerbated further.

It is widely agreed that a reduction of school class sizes is long overdue and here, politicians have abrogated the responsibility to present and future generations. The British people have been fed an image of themselves as wallowing in laziness. Such an image is a gross misconception of the fact. It is high time the British public cease believing in politicians who portray images of knowing it all. Such arrogance should be treated with the contempt it deserves.

Is it therefore so surprising that young people have taken to the streets recently in such a disturbing reaction to their betrayal by the political elite? There are so many things that are coming out every day. Look at those students that were protesting; they were given promises only seven months earlier that they would not be "saddled with debts." Now they find that these promises were not what they were made out to be and there was certainly no mention of increasing students' fees at the time. So how much should you believe of these people who aspire to high office? I mean; then, they were saying that students shouldn't be saddled with debts; but now they are heaping more debts on them.

So I think to myself, is it really worth listening to these people when they want to get into high office? It's just like when you read a newspaper. You see, I do not have any affiliation to any particular newspaper. I will read one paper one day, then another on another day. Then I form my own opinion. Like how the government is cutting back on new schools, but does nothing to stop benefit cheats. I have seen people who are supposed to be disabled, but they have a holiday every year. I don't mean going away for a few days - no, these people are going abroad. And not only that; there are people in this country who haven't done a day's work in donkey's years, yet they are living better than us working people. I don't understand a system that allows this.

Neither do I understand Britain's Open Door policy to immigrants from the EU because such an influx will have profound consequences. People are coming to a small country; one of the most densely populated in Europe. And the enduring power of such a European tide, which has effectively positioned Britain on the back foot, will - if not checked - sweep away our last vestiges of sustainable productivity.

Little wonder migrants of various descriptions see my beloved Britain as a soft touch.

There are plenty of authentic British migrants. Also there are plenty who are British only when they want to falsify Britishness to their favour. The British hierarchy are unrealistic; wasting time, energy and hard cash pandering to some in a vain effort to transform them to the genuine article. Out of the two dozen or so countries that make up the European Union, Britain has for a long time been at the economic vanguard.

People of grass root cultivation are very much aware of the discrepancies between imagery and the gulf that exist with visual. That is to say; the politicians see it one way, but the underprivileged see it in an entirely different way. Those in power just don't know that the immigrants that now flock to our shores are taking them for a ride. We see it. We hear for ourselves what these newcomers are saying. We can see that these people will never conform to our way of life.

So I, for one, am in harmonious agreement with the concept of large scale reduction in migrant numbers. The list of problems in dealing with such issues is much more of a poison chalice then where some seem to find satisfaction in only referring to non-EU immigrants. The electorate is very much aware of the need to find such gratification a mutual Badge of Honour; one for putting in place a scheme simply to appease other ministerial appetites. That is, those in power want to be honoured by trying to pretend that they are tackling immigration.

Such exhilaration is likely to be short lived. Most people intending to travel to Britain are well aware of the existence of a common order of Governance that in itself makes Britain a magnet and a favourable travel destination. There are indeed valid reasons why Britain should be the undoubted favourite for a more flexible system rather than just up-holding the rule of law. Indeed, they should become a more vigorous defender of the status quo. No longer should we British be lectured about various guidelines on diversity and equal opportunity, even though they are at the forefront on our core values.

But still we hear the rebuttal from spineless aspirants of high office that, "They come over here; pay their taxes ..." expecting the knowledgeable public to nod agreement on misplaced optimism. It seems that Britain, by its very system of laws and taboos, is in a comatose state; oblivious to the prevailing current which should be of grave concern to the system.

So this nation, that prides itself in democracy, free speech, and honesty; and where others marvel at the exploits of the British Bulldog Spirit, now finds within it a huge number of ordinary people who are, by the very country they love, being deterred from being truthful. Are we now staring at a new phenomenon that is creating confusion by castigating anyone attempting to be forthright? In retrospect the community should adopt the methods and habits of some politicians who have recently been specialising in selective honesty. Trust them at your peril. You may come to realise they assume the shape of straight bananas.

But not all; I salute the Right Honourable Mr Jack Straw and the comments made by the reputable Mr Calvin Mackenzie. Forthright, honest and brave; they speak what the Silent Majority know to be truthful. And I Myself, as a black man, I am quite aware there is a considerable number of English people who show great restraint by not coming out into the open; fearing they will be ostracised in Britain because, by following the laws of taboo, you will avoid a certain turbulent passage in any discussion on this issue.

It is very noticeable, this lack of fluidity during utterance; choosing their words with care and apprehension, like ill equipped service personnel on their first mission to Helmand Province seeking IED explosives. Yet in so doing, practitioners of the status quo unwittingly safeguard the detection of heinous characters in Britain. There is a prevailing culture where elements of some communities need to be exposed for their misdeeds. Yet no matter how unsavoury these characters are, they are still allowed to spread their poisonous propaganda unfettered by the British Establishment.

We see it all the time; people from abroad manipulating our system in various ways. No matter what prospect of toxic cocktails our misguided system absorbs. They commit crimes here, which - in their own country - would see them tried, condemned and executed all on the same day. Yet here, we provide funds from the public purse to mount a defence that sees them often acquitted of all wrongdoing.

And the more the world becomes destabilized, so the more people turn up on our doorstep expecting us to keep them. Often they claim to be fleeing from rebels, but when this cannot be justified they talk about suffering from a lack of democracy. Well, we know that they are economic migrants, even though they claim that they are being tortured because they have some political affiliation and they want to exercise their human rights. And then we have to give them the money to fight us in our own courts for their 'right' to settle here.

Now why is this? Take those two war criminals Radovan Karadzic and Ratko Mladic. It didn't take the Serbs long to pack them both off to The Hague. Mladic, for example, went within a week of his court appearance. So why is it that the UK can't do the same? No; we still house them and feed them. Then, because kids are not supposed to be kept in detention, we allow their parents to remain at large. Well you can see the good that that does when seventy-five thousand of them suddenly disappear from the radar. What were the authorities expecting? That they were going to come and tell us that their time's up and to please deport them? I don't think so.

You can see that our system needs to be changed. Look at that hook-handed fundamentalist cleric Sheikh Abu Hamza al Misri, who, as The Spectator noted way back on the 15th March 2003 was, "The most loathed man in Britain." Yet, when his congregation was blocking the pathway, we even gave him police protection. He must have thought that our system is insane. But if you or I were to get together outside with five or six others, the police would soon be there moving us on. Yet, if the American hadn't asked us to apprehend Hamza, he'd still have his freedom and would no doubt still be carrying on cursing us. We didn't even want to send him back to his own country. He's originally from Jordan and they've still got the death penalty. Well so what? That's his country we're talking about. What's that got to do with us? No; it's time we shrugged off our saintly garments of political correctness.

5 A TESTIMONY TO DESPERATION

Now another trait that I have noticed, and it is one that sets us apart from the rest of the European Community is when we use the phrase, 'Jack of all trades; master of none.' But the world is a changing world. It has always changed and it will continue to do so. Therefore we should not keep specialising in one particular field to earn a living. Instead, we should be adaptable. Then if one trade does not work and another one comes to the fore, there will be a better chance for us to get something from the one that's doing better.

This necessity to change is evident from the way technology is forever out-dating our skills. Because although technology has been of great benefit to mankind, it is a misplaced belief to let it be regarded as a panacea. During an unbroken period of technological brilliance, mankind has been in awe of mind boggling feats that have become an integral part of our daily lives. And although investors have reaped rich rewards, the yawning abyss between the rich and poor remains as wide as ever. Now, since we all aspire to a measure of opulence, we beg the question, "Why are so many experiencing no more than a frugal existence?" Analysing our knowledge in this scenario; the answer lies in their virtues of wisdom.

You see, technology is just like the waves coming out of the ocean. It brings with it a lot of debris to the shores and when it recedes, the debris is left high and dry. And make no mistake; we the workers - we are the debris. It's a fact; even though it may bring a touch of sadness, we may feel glum when we, in our moments of solitude, ponder the hard facts. But it is inescapable. Because we are constantly striving for technology and technology is conflicting with mankind. There is a major conflict between technology and mankind. What happens is that the people with the money; they go for technology. Now, they're not thinking in terms of the effect of laying-off two-hundred and fifty people who used to do a job when they can get the machinery which only needs twelve people to run it. And the path of technology is moving in such a way that sooner or later there will be less mechanics. They already have computers that tell you what's wrong. All a mechanic now needs to do is replace the faulty part. The computer will tell them which part needs changing. And, as for the part, these are being made by robots.

So when we talk about technology the more we are talking about the scrap-heap of people themselves. We are the scrap-heap. Technology is fine - to a certain extent. That is why I have said that we need to have a different type of revolution. People's attitude, people's thinking, people who - once they have made sufficient cash - must see that there is no need to hoard so much of it. Instead, they should be assisting people; giving them better wages down the line.

Now if we continue with this process of growth, even though certain sections of our manufacturing industry are creating a world first and becoming pioneers in their chosen art of modern science, it does not yield a great deal of benefit to the nation as a whole. Not, that is, unless we can be creative to the point where we can have greater mass involvement of human resources. Otherwise it is not real growth. The bright spots - dazzling as they are - the area they brighten is not sufficient to compensate for the vast number languishing in modern Britain.

Therefore, if the politicians speak, and claim to be duty-bound when they stand in front of the nation, and deliver what is supposed to be information that is meant to brighten the lives of the nation as a whole, how much sincerity lies within that duty and knowledge and optimism and aspiration? Because you will still find that those bright spots are bright only in certain areas. We are told, "Two and a half percent growth in the economy," but do we see this? It is almost meaningless; it's non-existent; it does not brighten up our lives, all we see is greyness stretching out into the distance. In reality, how much optimism should we place on the people who we vote for to place us into a better future when right now vast numbers of the population feel on the receiving end? There are not too many clear answers that we get. We get a lot of ambiguity, which does not inspire our confidence.

The new forms of production coming out of our manufacturing industries; we've still got to remember - they are still the children of technology. The more technology we have; the less human resources are used. If we go back to the post-war age, the world has made vast improvements in science, engineering and technology. We have seen the introduction of man-made satellites launched into space and ICBMs (Intercontinental Ballistic Missiles). Since then, we have seen man set foot on the moon and we've seen aircraft able to go into space and return without disintegrating. In more recent times there have been further advances, with the ingenuity of man allowing him to fly into space and coming back, landing on air strips. For example, the space shuttle, which was used many times over, and also medicine, which has been improved no end by modern science. Indeed, medical science has, with its advances in transplants and so forth, liberated us from the effects of many complaints that fifty years ago would have been fatal.

However, at the same time the world has been growing hungrier. On each occasion of austerity measures, the greatest victims have been human costs. So stunted has been our recovery that we fail to attain that which was previous there, because technology is here to stay. So, how should we be measuring growth? What are the tell-tale signs that indicate growth? When we talk about percentages we think of the economy. It is no good; we keep pointing only to the bright spots saying, "Well, our parents didn't get this and they managed." But now we have vast numbers that fail to obtain any measure of opulence. The world is getting more and more difficult to manage because the very same technology assists them to be more aware of what is missing. The Television; the mobile phone; the Blackberry: comparing from their own dire situation to positions of the elite in other parts of the globe.

We face huge challenges in obtaining resources. The planet is crying out.

Our water system is getting to be a bit dicey. And yet we are the main contributors to the malaise of the natural environment. Yet still, we continue to go more and more into technology for the benefit of the rich and powerful. Is it not time for mankind to come together? No longer should we find individuals having the wanton privilege of holding excessive well-being. Because when you are doing that, a lot is going to one corner. And while some people are enjoying great privilege, the rest of us can't come up - you have to stay down. From the cradle to the grave, you stay that way; because - no matter how you try - too many things conspire against you. It's the way the System works. So you never get out of it; one or two members of a family may climb up, but in the main they only climb to a certain level -they can't go beyond that. And in some households they all end up being in dissent with the establishment. Then they lose their aspirations; they lose motivation; what else can they do? The young see their parents working hard yet never moving from south to north of the economic divide.

For instance, you see someone who's worth fifty billion pounds. But what did he do for his fifty billion pounds? Look, there are more millionaires and more billionaires than there probably were twenty years ago - but that doesn't mean that there is prosperity. It's only for a few, but it should not be only the preserve of the minority. It should be more widespread, then you would find people would have greater contentment they would not be so rebellious. You keep getting this the world over. 1 mean, people might see other people commit a robbery and they turn a blind eye. You become part of the system.

It's like a tiger in the jungle. If it sees a human being it doesn't mind eating that person because it's a battle of survival. It's not a question of doing bad; it's a way to survive. People know it is wrong but to them it becomes normal because this is the only avenue left to them. So, a lot of people with opulence - it is not like years gone by - they have become prisoners in their own home. They've got iron gates because they need to see who is there. This means that they no longer have that total mental freedom now they have reached a certain level within society. You see, you or 1 could go out any time; we don't need no bodyguard. But when you have that level of opulence you've got to be careful. You could be robbed, you could be deprived of your health - it could even be fatal.

Now I mentioned earlier how difficult it is for poorer families to move from south to north; and I don't mean loading a removal van and heading away from London pass the Watford Gap Service Station on the M1. I mean crossing the social equator that divides rich and poor. Imagine, for a moment, the World Trade Centre's towers before their demise. They were each 110 stories high. Now think of a line drawn across them on the 55th Floor. If all the families in Britain could be housed in those towers, most would be below the 55th Floor, with the poorest on the ground floor. Those floors above would be less and less crowded until the highest floors were hardly populated at all - just the richest in those.

Well, that line on the 55th floor is like the social equator - think of the twin towers now as a map. Above being north and below being south. So in modern parlance the pronouncement of economy is a sounding joy to those north of the social equator whenever the results are deemed to be favourable. And it is refreshing to hear a spokesperson for the political elite using the cliché, "They have their eye on the ball." Still, considering there is a north - south divide it would be a more appropriate consideration for them to be, "Having eyes on more than one ball." This is because, "Economy," by name can - and is - a lop-sided subject when it comes to, "Where the benefit goes."

Today, the promise of recovery and growth is hugely superficial. Some members of the electorate may find such a promise intensely stimulating because people tend to feel better by listening and hearing some of the stuff they wish to hear. Cynical to the electorate's knowledge, in Britain the system has lost control. A raging war within the British system's own bedroom has resulted in sliding the scale of military might in a downward trajectory.

We say that we are adjusting to the modern era, but really we're simply trying to do the best we can. Take Bulgaria; they had Harrier Jump Jets, but they've been phased out. And even what used to be our "Eyes and ears" - the Nimrod; they've been grounded. We have even joined forces with the French because we no longer have a proper navy of our own.

Since we lost the empire we have lost our industrial base. We have slipped down quite immensely; never to go back to the top. Because what we are doing now is pushing innovation. I do believe we will have a recovery; but not up to former days. We just don't have the ability. That's because our industrial base has gone forever. We have to rely on our enemies for our energy. All the gas and oil is getting harder to extract.

It's only in banking and tourism where we are still doing well; but these won't last forever. The Chinese, and even the Indians, will soon take over the Banking Sector of the world. We are a high tax economy, whereas they have low tax. So when we talk about export, in real terms, we are not doing well. Other nations are going for the Lion's share. Innovation, science; these once used to be done by British people, but now it is foreign people who are the pioneers. These people go wherever it suits them. It could very well be economic factors, it could be taxation. The fact is we have nothing else except banking to depend on.

Not too many years ago we used to talk about how many cars we used to export and how many we import. Then we use to export more than we imported because we had many plants. But now the balance between exported and imported cars has changed. And anyway, the plants in Britain are now foreign owned. So, if we keep going on this trend, where are we going to be in five years time? We use to do ship building, we lost that. All the shipyards are closed. The coal mines are closed. It is very visual now; signs that tell us for the next twenty years - the omens are not good.

Take a look at our high streets; we've already seen that the biggest is the fittest. These are the undoubted survivors. You walk through almost any town in Britain and you will see the proliferation of small businesses. But how, one wonders, do they survive? Because we have come to experience in more recent years, and it is still broadening ever wider, that the major players of our high streets have become almost like eczema on the human skin. Everywhere you go there are new supermarkets springing up. They are almost appearing daily. And they are cornering the market.

Now they may make big announcements about creating employment. One recently announced that it will create seven and half thousand jobs over the following year. But wait! How many of these jobs are part-time? And if these jobs are part-time, can the people make a realistic living out of it? Can they look forward to a brighter day? How many of them, doing these sorts of jobs, can say that their existence is not simply frugal? But these people, like everyone else, have desires to better themselves. However, these are just low paid jobs and it's really hard to make a decent living in them. Many supermarket workers haven't had a holiday in years. So what happens? Their children are more likely to grow up delinquent. This is because of the environment in which they are brought up. It is not particularly conducive to their development.

So, when we look at a lot of these expanding businesses we pay scant regard to the frequency of small businesses closing down. The cream is being extracted by those big shops on the high streets. Every quarterly period we hear that profits are announced by these big shops and, almost without fail, these monopolies increase their profits; but you can bet your bottom dollar that there has been a whole host of small shops closing down.

Seeing the new shops opening is testimony to desperation. Because in reality, if you don't know which way to turn then all this scenario presents, in any country - any community, is simply a battle to survive. And there is bound to be lots happening that will contravene the status quo. People are more likely to look for other ways to survive. Even if they know the difference between right or wrong. Survival will be the central piece of the action; whether it be fraud, drugs or buying stolen goods. So, in effect, you are creating your own Taliban - because you can never defeat them. Their hearts and minds will never be won.

Yet what prospects have we got; just cut-backs to reduce the Budget Deficit? And are these cuts here to stay? If they are, then high unemployment is also here to stay. Now there is a trend that is emanating from the government, that we work more for less. So, if more for less becomes permanent then what impact will this have on society? People can only bear so much for so long. But eventually you will have a vacuum. And that's why you see that what is happening in other parts of the world is now happening here.

6 DIGNITY IN THE FACE OF ADVERSITY

On the sixth of August 2011 we were living witnesses to a spectacle of an impious alliance. Without any acting, the non-participating community watched in horror the real London Burning. Without any morals, pride, or dignity; such insidious developments - so symptomatic and wicked - reveals the crassness of mental degradation. It is shameless and shallow; even a member of the legal profession tried to attempt mounting a defence for such activity. It was notable for the toxic excuses propagated by many who had deluded themselves into believing that they had a case - citing that they want their tax back. This beggars belief; viewing such undignified individuals who by sheer image do not appear to have managed a single working day in their life. However, seeking to solve any alternative reason is just as difficult as finding a solution.

The propensity to be consistently associated with violence appears never to be in short supply and seems to joyfully extend as a fashion into notoriety. And the ability to avoid controversy or violence is not part of their chosen art. Is it by coincidence, just to name these few, when almost every day brings a tragedy linked with violence in what is now regarded as just another day? We then saw, during and towards the end of the Notting Hill Carnival, the highest percentage of teenage fatalities in the capital. Therefore I say to all perpetrators and defenders, "Speak in one voice. Spring Clean the image; gain a good measure of integrity and follow the Road of Redemption.

Nowhere can we find a more stunning example of such a determined spirit than in Nelson Mandela. I have made mention of him already in this book; of his imprisonment and resolve. He earned respect. Those we saw on our television screens - either committing acts of barbarism, or revelling in the outcome afterwards - do not respect themselves. They are to be kept at arm's length. The trouble they cause is because they have no self control; they lack a plan for their lives. They are - in short - controlled by a different spirit. They are the ones who get into drugs and mess up their lives and, as we so graphically saw, the lives of others.

Yet these are the very people who complain and claim they are marginalised. No - they marginalise themselves. They are quick to criticize but they don't appreciate the chances they've squandered. Now, one of my best friends in this country is an Irish man. He used to have a club in the West End, near China Town. It's not a place I go often but he still sends me Christmas cards. He used to have a club in Dalston. A friend of mine asked if I'd do some security, and I went to his club. That's where I first met him. But at the time the club was not doing well. However, he still had to pay his overheads and his staff. Well, I could see that he wasn't getting in many customers, so I said, "Just give me my cab fare". I wouldn't take any pay from him. I was the only one who didn't take wages. Then he got new DJ's in and business perked up.

So, you see, life's not all about grabbing what you can get or wanting what someone else has without working hard like they did to get it. Once, during the time that I was a self-employed builder, I took a two-week holiday in the USA. But just before I went, I had a chance encounter with a New Zealander who'd just come back from a 6-month spell there. This guy gave me the name of someone he'd worked for while in Boston. So when I got there, I found the place where the New Zealander had worked and asked to see the manager. The receptionist asked me to waitand after a while the manager came out. I told him who I wanted to speak to; this was his boss - he owned a whole string of businesses. Well, the manager rang his head office and got me an appointment. I went straight there and was soon being interviewed by the Main Man. He was so taken by me - Americans see through people; if you're bold and take the initiative they appreciate that - he offered me a job; just like that. I said if I ever come over for longer, I'd take him up on his offer.

You see, you've got to be bold. While I was in Boston, I visited Filene's Department Store which at the time was the biggest store they had. I soon realized that I was the only black person in the whole building. Anyway, undeterred, I asked a sales assistant about some perfume that was for sale. Noticing that I was not local she asked where I came from. Well, on telling her, "London Town," she quickly called over the other assistants who all asked excitedly if I knew Prince Charles. It just so happened that at that moment he was visiting nearby Harvard College. They all became so enthusiastic about getting my name and phone number I was lucky to get away unscathed.

But, it's all about attitude. I get so disappointed with young people who mouth off to the police when they - the young people - are blatantly in the wrong. Now, in my younger days, I would speed everywhere; but if the police pulled me up I would acknowledge my mistake. And I was always being stopped. Until one time, that was; it must have been over twenty-five years ago now. I'd taken the turning to Hackney at the Bow Flyover on two wheels. My wife and her sister were in the car and the police pulled me over. It was early in the morning - I'd just finished for the night and I was still in my bouncers' uniform; that is dark suit and bow tie. But, as usual, I was polite. I got out of the car and smiled at the police officer. Seeing that I'd been working the door he simply asked if I would think of the safety of my passengers. He was right and I have never transgressed since.

Reasoning should be an art of human instinct. When you personify a lack of such basic normal standards you detach yourself from human understanding. The best element of respect belongs to self-esteem. Such an element in your civil cabinet is undoubtedly a priceless possession. When your glory relates only to the present there will be no reward for the future. Take, for example, Mr Jahan of Winson Green. Now, by the manner he conducted himself in the face of adversity – calm, dignified and humble - it earned him the respect he deserves.

He was, you may recall, the father of one of the men killed while they were protecting property during the riots of August 2011. Yet, although being the victim of a wanton act of barbarism, his civility no doubt helped to quell the potential of violent reaction. In so doing, it revealed his character as having the steadfast personification of reasoning of the highest order. This is a direct challenge to any group as to what lessons they have learned.

Now Mr Jahan is the epitome of a shining example not simply to his ethnic group but to the much wider arena. His courage adds immense beauty to the ideal of social cohesion. Any development of an insidious nature running counter to such cohesion will be the recipient of the label it deserves. For such occurrences are not news in isolation; they hold major implications for our entire world.

Would it have been such a bad idea for some of the people interviewed on national TV, whether perpetrators or defenders, to have demonstrated sincere recognition towards those touched by such tragedy? For it is in these traumatic times that those - who, behaving in such exemplary manner within the immediate aftermath - should be offered genuine condolence. But why should anyone group cry wolf with greater monotony than others? Is this merely haphazard? Are the African-Caribbean group more vulnerable? Should they wonder at being more disliked when they have a greater track record of carrying offensive weapons? They seem to delight in the unsociable image they portray; attending similar schools and having, per capita, an over-all dismal performance of attainment. If any prescription is to be found and administered the human sense must be specific in its detail. It would be most welcome for groups, of any description, to be real - not heaping on to others what should be their very own responsibility. In other words, demonstrate that they are moving towards the refinement of their attitude.

Not that all their grievances are without justification; far from it. The reaction which flared first in Tottenham cannot be judged in isolation. And here I am not - and never will - make excuses for blatant wrong doing. It was criminality personified. I do however go along with the initial concern, when the news came out that Mr. Duggan was fatally wounded, because of what has transpired over a 30 year period leading up to the events of the 4th August 2011. Because, having read some of the proceedings within the English legal system, I have attempted to equate the system with the public and their deeds and misdeeds - trying to draw a parallel. And I have found, in so doing, that there are gross discrepancies.

We start with Steven King; going back approximately thirty years, who was shot somewhere in Chelsea. He was thought to be a terrorist but subsequently it turned out that he was not. He was given sufficient bullets which would have rendered him obese by the virtue of metal they supplied him, even though his body was only partially inside the car and the rest on the outside. Well, it was obvious that no cop was trying to arrest him. These are sources for simmering discontent.

Then we had the Brazilian who was thought to be a terrorist and it was stated, "He was given a number of bullets." Well, I suppose the first two or three were probably sufficient to be fatal. So, if the alleged number of bullets from official circles was correct, then we could deem this to be "over-the-top." Therefore, if this was beyond the limits of reason, we have to ask serious questions which require serious answers. That is; from that perception, what should we require to be reasonable force?

We also had the woman in Tottenham in the early '80s whom the police sought to arrest who was deemed to be an illegal immigrant. Yes, it was right for the cops to move in and detain her. But after the cops moved in -

we may recall - she did not live to breathe another day. We also had an incident in Victoria Park Road, not too long ago, when the police were fed by a report, apparently, that a man was seen walking up the road with a gun. He was blatantly shot dead and it was proven that he did not have anything more lethal wrapped up than a table leg.

So how can we balance these incidents? Why haven't those issues been addressed correctly? Why has there been what appears to be consistent hogwash? Even if there is no wholesale protest on the streets, it doesn't hide the fact that tempers are frayed. It puts certain sections and elements of the system in very poor light. And there are many more which do not need to be mentioned but the system can find them within their own archives.

So how many people have died in police custody? That is; without proper genuine explanation as to why. And those deceased, prior to the loss of life, were in the care of servants of the establishment. It would be good to see sections or representatives of the establishment come out before us, the people, and attempt to address these issues. F air should be fair. Simply because some have gone down, or probably asphyxiated, by representatives of the establishment, without logical reason, it should not be construed as, "A life that was not worth living."

On the other hand, when members of the public are hauled before the courts, we have seen, on numerous occasions, where the judges deemed that those members of the public - in these particular instances - did not use reasonable force. Now, we have to bear in mind that those members of the public who are on trial at those given times are not necessary trained or possess any physical back-up in case their intent to subdue did not succeed. When confronted by an assailant it is very rare, if not at all, that they have good intentions. And it is almost a hundred percent, when you are under attack or your privacy has been flouted, that those elements provoking you have no regard for your safety.

Take for example Tony Martin, the farmer who was imprisoned because he shot a would-be burglar at night. And this burglar was not alone. Yet Mr Martin was imprisoned because he was deemed to have not used reasonable force. But administering the concepts and laws of the land should, at all times, be even-handed. I mean; when last did we ever hear of attacks by the police on parts of the public at large where judges claim that police used excessive force? Does this mean that the police can use force with impunity. Even in Mr Duggan's case, the initial news had to be corrected by the Independent Police Complaints Commission (IPCC) who admitted that there was no evidence that the deceased fired a gun.

We, the public, have to ask serious questions: why was it alleged that the deceased had fired a gun? Was this an attempted cover-up? Did the police - who are trained to carry out certain tasks - when confronted, panic in sheer terror? Was it a case of safety first rather than fulfilling the task that they were trained to execute? It should be palpably clear, to the people who represent us at the upper levels of society, that these issues should be brought onto the table for grown civilised people to try to correct these concerns.

Yet keeping them covered and then simply having them hog-washed is not the answer.

The youths out there - while you've got to deal with them justifiably severely - should be shown that you are even-handed. Show them that, when you have officers who panic and overdo it, they get justified criticism and, even though to some extent I sympathise with the officers, punished for any calculable wrongdoing. It is unthinkable to have so many people who have lost their lives in inexplicable circumstances, or even explainable circumstances, and for no one to be held accountable.

7 POLISHING-UP THE IMAGE

Irrespective of how much we condemn the tactics of law enforcement, justifiably so, we must also admit that there is a lot of ignorance out on the streets. There are, we know, lots of people in the African-Caribbean community with a great deal of integrity and pride, but their influence is being undermined by those who have no pride and who do not mind parading a lack of integrity. This is sheer ignorance. It would be not a bad idea to get a team of some of the people who have sunk beneath the gutter and bring them to the exposure of television and get them to speak honestly; asking them various questions and waiting for them to give you their answers.

The majority of them, who perpetrated and paraded those evil onslaughts on decent hard-working members of our community, would be put into a corner by the very questions being asked of them. And whether they have been born and bred in this country or have come to this country at a very early age, question them about what happened to the schooling they had. We should find out from them, in their own words and irrespective of whether we agree or disagree, because it is good to allow them simply to air what they have got to say about it. But no doubt about it; this does not necessary mean that what they have to say will be added to their status quo. We will have to do like the judges; after we have heard, and we have asked all the relevant questions, then we give a summing up of how people of rational behaviour behave and ought to behave.

We need to ask them; what are their grievances about? We want to know, and if they mention, "No jobs," then we should take time in a calm measured manner to ask of them what sort of jobs are they looking for. And then, should they say anything, ask them - on a certain level of skill -

are they qualified to do that? If they say, "Yes," ask them to prove that, because they have got to have a paper of some sort. Then move on, asking how old are they, how long since they left school and how many jobs have they had – if they had any ~ and what sort of jobs were they?

In this way we are showing them that they have to come clean because lies would not be acceptable. Then we should ask them one of the key questions; "What are they doing to alleviate the problem or have they done anything to alleviate the problem?" It is no good having a war of words with them, we should be getting them to see that when they say that they would do anything, that they have the necessary skills. You can't just apply for a job without having the right qualifications or experience.

Also, we should ask how they expect to look after themselves and, if they have any children, how do they expect their families to be looked after. Then, having said that, put it to them, "Do they believe it is because of prejudice or discrimination? Is this the reason why they feel such desperation? Are they aware that they are not the only ethnic group in the country? What do they think of these other groups? How are the other groups doing? Do they believe the other groups are being given greater preference than they are; if so - what?

Remember that this group is on television. It is not just this little group, and the studio audience, that are being faced with reality. There will be the wider group of like-minded individuals out there watching. So you will be sending a message to them as well, that there are things out there that they should be doing; things they haven't tried. Have they, for instance, thought of getting any more qualifications since leaving school? If they say, "No," then why do they think they came out of school without any qualifications? Ask them, "What do they believe should be done?" or, if they dilly dallied at school, what sort of reflections have they had - if they had any; and how long are they going to go on in this manner? That is; to perpetuate this culture of doing nothing. We need to find out from them just what, exactly, are they expecting from society.

Now, if they say what they expect; ask them how do they expect to obtain it? Because if you are claiming, "No employment," and that you are bored well, I was your age once; but I was getting out of bed at five in the morning, running for the bus to start work at six. So don't let any youngster tell me they are bored. I find the world a wonderful place - it's a pity I can only live for a couple of hundred years at the most. There's so much to see, so many places to go; and so much learning I'd like to do. But they say they're bored - they need to be more adventurous, more enterprising.

Well, anyway, have they given any thought to advertising? When they look at a vehicle in a showroom and it looks very neat and tidy; does it look attractive to them as well - what do they believe about image? How do they view their own image; how saleable is it? How marketable is it to a prospective buyer?

After coming out of this discussion would they be willing to consider their image? Do they believe image can be of good assistance if you appeal to prospective employers? This culture of walking about hooded and scarved to conceal facial identity; how do they believe it is viewed by other sections of the wider community?

How comfortable do they feel; or confident, or clever, in behaving in that manner? Such conduct is a detachment for people of rational thinking. So, putting it to them; how, when all is said and done, do they feel for the people who have lost their businesses and who are in state of despair? What would they like to say to them? And what would they like to say to mates, or like-minded people? Do they believe that they have won any particular benefit from their exploits of what the nation - and the world - came to witness with such horror; particularly those in the African-Caribbean community. Don't they realise it has taken them down a few more notches? When people see them out in public, performing in that manner, and the images they portray in their performance - would they imagine how they are viewed? Do they believe people are not justified to view them with serious suspicion when the image and action is not conducive to the human good?

It would be far better to move out of that quagmire. Some of them already have children and those that haven't, will sooner or later have their very own. Would they like their own ones to follow in their footsteps? Or do they believe this is the best preparation for the ones who are to succeed them? Would they mind giving an example of how they want their own life to move on? Would they like to persist on the present course? Should they say, "No," then what would they do to alter that? What do they believe they should have been doing? Do they believe they have learned any lessons as a consequence of what happened? Would they like to say anything to the government, or the system as a whole? If so, what would they like to say?

Finally, would they like to prepare the ground in a more productive manner for their own future generation? What would they like the future generation to have for a better life? And would they take that into consideration before they continue to transgress any further? I wonder if their answers could stand the final analysis of such a discussion. Probably not, in my early years

I may have come across discrimination, but never in my adult life. But then you are bound to get a certain element in every society. This is just human nature. But often we can over-react to just everyday misunderstandings.

I remember one day I was on my way from B&Q and I had a tub of paste. I was about to get on a bus when the driver stopped me. I asked why and he said that paint was not allowed. I lifted the tub so he could see it was paste and he said, "Come in". Now I believe that he made an error of judgement and we are all prone to errors so I should not judge him for that. I, myself, tend to be very meticulous in whatever I chose to say and how I act. This is because I am highly disciplined. But sometimes I hear people talking about ethnic differences and I pull them up. I tell them; if they go to the Caribbean they will get the same thing and they have to listen to me because they hold me in high respect.

For example; one day I was at a Networking Meeting in the Spotted Dog, Barking and there was a lady who had overheard me talking. Then when I sat down she said, "What do you do?" and mentioned that she had been taking note of what I had been saying. She told me that she was a senior lecturer at the University of East London and asked if I would come and give a lecture to the undergraduates there. She was a senior psychologist there. Now I have spoken a few times at other colleges. One was to pupils at a school in Mile End Road, another was at the City and East London College in Stepney; also the Rotary Club of Great Britain in East India Dock Road.

And I tell them what I think: you get a lot of people going to colleges and universities and some of the subjects are almost useless. This is because some qualifications are never going to give much employment for any lengthy period. They are just soft options; allowing those that study them an easy ride through higher education. So why acquire a degree that sounds good? They should be doing much more than this, to make it worth their time. Yet you'll get them say that they are going to college to learn 'Tourism and Travel'. So I ask them, "Why Tourism and Travel alone?" In today's world this is grossly inadequate; you should also add languages because by having languages your world has become more international. And now it's a much more diverse world. Tourism and Travel? Tourism is not only people of your language. And travel? Well, you're not only travelling to people who speak your language. You are going to meet a mixture. So you've got to keep looking to broaden your scope. You've got to keep looking for that. This means that some degrees are not worth the paper they're written on; because you can't get work.

I put it to them straight; that the reason so many people go to college these days to study such subjects as 'Tourism and Travel' is just to socialise. They are not really doing any hard graft. These people are living in a daydream. These qualifications are not going to get you work. It could be that you are English, and that's the only language you speak. While you have the time, while you don't have any responsibilities, you should be learning another two languages.

They should look at the trend of things; to see where people want to travel to the most.

Not to learn those languages like German or Spanish, because you get a lot of Germans or Spaniards that will compete for jobs with you. Now think about it. China has for a great length of time been closed to westerners; but no longer. Since the Beijing Olympics they have gone out of their way to welcome tourists. They've even opened up a massive office in Holborn just to process visas. Then there are places like The United Arab Emirates. Now that the oil has all but dried up, they have transformed places like Abu Dhabi; making them havens of holiday resorts. So why not learn Arabic, Japanese or Chinese - places where people speak less English. Then, if you were to learn these sorts of languages - make it a life-time ambition - you could really go places. You can work for them over there; you can work for them here. But young people don't see this; there are too many easy subjects. They go for these to their detriment.

8 GENEROSITY PERSONIFIED

Now it's one thing getting our young people to diversify, when seeking to obtain skills for their future well-being, and another to find jobs that will provide them with a livelihood. Because, with the cost of living spiralling higher and higher, the gap between Brits fortunate enough to be eking out an existence and those below the bread-line is widening, and sadly will continue to do so. The vast majority of the British People do have a high measure of common sense. Immigration in its proper form is not highly regarded as an issue. Yet we can plainly see that we still have a rapid population growth. We are declining one way and building up the other. We talk about capping non-EU migrants, but there is a case where we need them for development. Yet large numbers are coming here from Europe. So why? What are they doing, other than fanning?

And anyway, a lot of them are only using the farm as a stepping stone until they can move up to get a more comfortable living. So in other words, we are living beyond our means because we do not have the wealth to support all these people who are coming here. A lot of them have to "sign up". That is an additional burden. Even those that do work are low paid so their tax is insignificant. Therefore they get more out of us than we get from them. We get people from certain countries where they have large families. This means we have to find big houses for them and appropriate classes for their kids at schools and more doctors to look after them.

No wonder that we are being so over-stretched. And if we keep having these people coming in, then we need more houses. Then, should they commit crimes, more prison spaces. Yet our prisons are so full we can't send people to prison any more. Some of them become like the spongers we already have, and then we have to look after even more people. Well, we simply cannot afford it. We have to find places to build houses. Eventually we shall have to encroach on our 'Green Belts'.

On top of all this there's a housing crisis; I've been saying this for some time. Even the government has admitted that they don't know how they are going to build homes to satisfy the needs of the people. Furthermore, are the government confident that they could give a credible assessment of the population growth ten years from now? Housing is currently being built at the lowest rate for 90 years. I would be interested to know; will the pace increase, and if so - to what extent? Do they know how many people are coming from mainland Europe and do they know the average birth-rate of these people? Then again; there are people travelling to the Asian sub-continent looking for lifelong partners; do they expect this figure to drop - and if they do - how? Are the government honest enough to admit if they have any power to influence this trend?

Yet, assuming these questions asked but with no positive answer to "Yes" - but more to the negative - then what sort of damage would we anticipate for Social Cohesion. These are important questions. And if these people keep on this trajectory, which appears remorseless, are we concerned or are we going to ignore it? Are we confident that we can turn the tide? Do we take into account the indigenous population of this country where we have large numbers on the housing waiting list? These people have been waiting many years and have no idea when they will be assisted.

I mean, who would get priority when our European counterparts arrive on these shores with families? Well, we know full well that when they arrive with kids, the authorities are looking to shelter them. Then, if the trend continues, how do you expect, within our own society, that we are not breeding discontent? Really, these are matters which require skilful and urgent attention. Mere platitudes are inadequate to quell the dissatisfaction which people rightly feel. Now, allied with a lower standard of living which is very much on the horizon, this will be bringing pressure to swathes of families. What sort of example will they be able to demonstrate to the up and coming ones? For it is the next generation that will no doubt feel they have a need for opulence. Why should they not have parity with those others who are enveloped in salubrious surroundings? But will they only be able to manage a frugal existence?

Even now our workers are being shunted out because of east European migrants. But, you might ask, if the immigrants are willing to work for low wages, why don't we? But look at their lifestyles. Do their kids all go to school? We don't want to fall to a level where our children end up roaming around creating mischief. No! We want our children to go to school, to be educated; to wear shoes and decent clothes.

Britain on the ropes, literally, where calling any respite off the ropes can only be obtained from the casualty department. What validity is there in the concept that talks, on one hand, about placing a cap from one section of the globe yet, on the other, allows people the length and breath of Europe to come and go at their own convenience? Such tide of ebb and flow creates its own current. The whole concept, irrespective of what was initially envisaged, is not conducive to the intended purpose. It has been well documented that it created a shock to the nation's pulse. Such vast numbers arriving from the mainland is unprecedented.

Critical analysis of the human mind should have been operational. Think of how accommodation was obtained. I will give you an example; one million immigrants come here in a short space of time. Did we have a housing programme? The answer is no. So, they end up cramped together - sharing accommodation. Well, those who were first given this accommodation are now reaping the benefits by sub-letting. And where are these people living? Because so many came in between 2004 - 2009, they will all be sharing similar postcodes. This is very common; lots of people all with the same postcode.

Now, within the corridors of knowledge, one should be able to organise a level of experience. There are issues of fascination for the establishment to supply its digestive organs. You know, launch an investigation. Find out why so many have the same postcode. With the advent and the use of technology, if various segments of the establishment are to adequately perform their duties, they should be able to find - within the congested post code areas - how many foreign nationals are now living there and from what sections of the globe and how recent have they been local.

Because, as I have alluded to previously, this is all to the detriment of the British worker.

This is because immigrants can be used as cheap labour. Not so long ago I went to Wicks near Seven Sisters Tube Station and I saw approximately 95 Eastern Europeans in total waiting there to be taken on for the day. It was so bad that Wicks' security called the police to move them on. Yet this goes on all the time. You can go to certain areas and see these people being picked up to do particular jobs; carpenters, bricklayers, plumbers, electricians, you name it. They'll pay a carpenter something like £70 for a day's labour. Well, a British carpenter would cost twice that. But then he is qualified. He has to pay tax. He will be paying the full going rate for whatever accommodation he has for his family. And while 1 do not dispute there are fine individuals, on arrival to Britain the system embarks on monumental efforts of welcome to give accommodation to new arrivals.

Well, such abounding warmth and hospitality are not very often reciprocated with genuine gratitude. Far from being good Samaritans to their compatriots, those immigrants who arrived earlier treat our acts of immense goodwill as a bonanza for them to strike lucky - cramming in lodgers for a quick kill with little objection from those who are desperate to melt within the system. Yet all this shelter and cash comes at the expense of the British taxpayer. It is, indeed, generosity personified.

So, it's little wonder that our country is on the ropes and wilting. Not, as we are, far away from the mainland; we therefore find ourselves in and at close quarters with our defences in tatters and our vulnerability exploited with consummate ease. Is there no way we can stop this flood of Eastern European immigrants? There are prevailing manifestations of our ethos, and related taboos, in Britain that stop us expressing publicly what is overwhelmingly felt and experienced by widespread knowledge. No one dare speak out. If someone was to mention this on a television chat show the presenter of the programme would slap them down. Other people would then say nothing, because people in general like to go with the flow.

It's a bit like how it used to be, not so very long ago, when a woman would go to the police to report being raped. Although she was the victim, she would be made to feel that it was her fault. Well, that's what people feel like now when they experience for themselves the harmful effects of immigration. They think, 'What's the point of raising the issue?' That leaves us very frustrated.

And why do we feel this? As part of the underprivileged; practical is the main instrument which guides our daily life. In every twist and turn we are confronted with reality not endowed with the trappings of vanity. From our standpoint we are not remote from the powers of nature. We are 'down-to-earth,' we see what is going on all around us. It is high time more true words should be spoken by the less, or the under privileged. We should be getting the politicians to start understanding us. We should ensure that those in power are listening sincerely to the voices of reason irrespective of class, creed or gender.

However this desire seems a vain hope. And as time goes by we are becoming more and more mistrustful of the upper class. Once we considered them sacrosanct; now we are more astute. Observing the processes of man and nature from the late sixties onwards we have come to witness the phenomenon of our most enduring challenger allied to the bravado and arrogance of some superficial intellectuals behaving like they were The Messiah. Be warned! If you take their preaching at breath value it will be to the detriment of your own observation. But there is no way for you to disagree with them. They expect you to be a passive listener. They have the whip hand.

9 NO SPIN ZONE

So, while being pummelled at home, how are we dealing with events on a world-wide scale? Because I find, in recent times, that people in general - when there's an election - are expressing the view of apathy and, as time evolves, it is gradually becoming clearer that whatever our leaders say has to be closely scrutinized. There are phrases being used for instance that, while giving a semblance of normality, are rather ambiguous.

As the story unfolds, more is being revealed of what was initially made up as an "intent" We find expressions used, as recent examples would demonstrate, such as: No Fly Zone and, Reform. Well, they are open to a multitude of adjustment because those expressions are deliberately used when the goal-posts are being moved. So when politicians use, "The Intent," it gives them room to manoeuvre.

Take for example the conflagration in Libya. We in Britain, our leaders at least, were backing hostility. Now a No Fly Zone, as it was originally defined, was to stop the perceived foe from getting combat aircraft airborne so as to negate them from embarking on wanton mayhem of their own people. But as events developed, we came to observe with quiet concern that our representatives were moving beyond the mandate which was accorded to them. Gradually they started to make their own interpretations. And what has now become palpably clear is that they were abusing the entrance that was given them by the UN. With no general opposition from the electorate, our leaders were gradually becoming more 'Cock-a-hoop'.

Yet we had previously been led to believe that outsiders should not embark on regime change. However, our leaders have become over-confident. Their deceit is revealing itself to us. Yet they keep hedging by insisting that,

"The opposing leaders are butchering their own people," - that they were embarking on a mission to protect 'the people under the cosh'. Now, looking at it from a wider perspective, it makes us wonder, what was the general aim? What was the real purpose of such missions?

We have heard from our own leaders, people we are supposed to look up to as examples of authenticity, adding further phrases such as: "We are looking after our own interests." So why was it not initially pronounced, in going to the UN for a mandate, that we were simply looking after our own interests? Rather than saying that it was because, "Their leaders are killing their own people." Because now it is clear that this was no more than a cynical ploy to bring us on board. Therefore, many people at large - making detailed studies of this - tend to reinforce their own belief that those leaders cannot be readily trusted. In so doing, while playing games with words and different games with actions, we the public are being educated in wanton cynicism.

Furthermore, it was pretty sad to see a delegation from our beloved country racing into Egypt immediately after the demise of Hosni Mubarak. And to lead a military delegation, When the people of that nation had yet to have a stable government, was grossly insensitive. Those unfortunate people, having recently experienced the rancour of upheaval Within their ranks, should have first been allowed a degree of stability. But no; instead we heard a shred-less excuse being offered by our representatives telling us that a programme of visits had been arranged in advance of the fall of Mubarak. I believe that our representatives had other priorities than the best interests of the Egyptian people. Are they so cynical as to expect us not to be aware that the delegation could have been postponed until a better time? Yet, even though ferocious hostilities had died down, there were still scores being settled in that country. So going with a huge delegation of military experts surely should not have been recommended as a highly political manoeuvre at that particular juncture. It would have been better to have got our priorities right and not charged in, seeking to supply them with military hardware.

Now, on top of that, we claimed to be assisting rebels openly and I very much doubt that this was within the UN mandate. This gives the appearance that, occasionally, we are making up the rules and regulations to suite our own ideals; even thriving on the fact that we gave an explanation which was not carefully thought out before, or even analysed after, as to its credibility or lack of it. For example; we embarked on the systematic destruction of military hardware while at the same time having our eyes on being a future supplier. So it looked like we had a conflict of interest. Was it really to assist the rebels; or was it to create employment back in our own homeland?

If we are so passionate in intervening whenever people are being systematically destroyed, or used by their leaders in power, are there not other areas of the globe where, like Libya, atrocities are taking place? We do not have very far to travel from Libya. For within the confines of the Middle East there is Bahrain. Here the Americans have a huge naval fleet and the US only offered mild words as a camouflage. Well, at least they said something - but when you look, there was never threat of action. Then we have the Yemen Peninsular where just as much savagery and blatant slaughter is being done to innocent civilians. But what action are we prepared to take to line this up uniformly with what we are doing in Libya?

So, the question is: are these principles selective? Would we be prepared to help the rebels in Syria? And, if so, in what shape or form would such help take? Have we spoken about a No-Fly Zone again, because we now know that the phrase 'No-Fly Zone' is open to various forms of interpretation as we move along the road to hostility while still seeking to lay claim to having a UN mandate.

It is very interesting to put into words the jingoism that some of our leaders used when they referred to Libya. Such as: "Step down;" "No further use in that particular country," "Time is not on its side." Did we use those same words in reference to the Yemini President; or Mr Asad of Syria? Those phrases were very conspicuous by their very absence. Are we going to see that this is a pattern that we are setting for future conflagrations of this type?

I very much doubt so; our venture into the Libyan campaign was always geared more towards an investment rather than an enforcement of the No Fly Zone. However, when you go in that round-about way, the world is watching. And this will only create renewed scepticism when you claim to be doing it for the best of reasons. There are a lot of activists around who will be wondering, "What are their true intentions?" Take the president of Zimbabwe, Mugabe, who very often uses propaganda to criticize Britain. You are giving him ammunition for some of the idiots to believe him. Now we know that Mugabe is nonsensical and we can ignore him, yet on the other hand take Ahmadinejad, the president of Iran. The western powers have been trying their level best to get him to give up his nuclear reactors. You think he will now, when he sees what's going on? Of course not! It will make him even more certain to keep his own nuclear weapons. And even those within Iran who are opposing him will come on board - so there will be less pressure on him to abandon the manufacture of nuclear armour. Because nuclear weapons are the sole guarantee that you will not be threatened by an external source.

So, while there may have been a short-term gain in Libya, you have to think of the greater consequences of it. For instance; they have tried lots of time to get North Korean to come on-board with nuclear disarmament. North Korea wanted to come to the conference table. But, just to get our hands on Gaddafi Oil, we have jeopardised this. Well, that oil was not coming here. We know that for a fact. It's also true that we have been talking to the rebels; making secret oil deals. So this fuels the suspicion that a lot of people already had about our intentions.

Now what about those countries yet to appear on the nuclear weapons' horizon? The Russians will help them; the Chinese will help them; even the Iranians might help them when they have the expertise. Had we forgotten this? We will never get rid of nuclear weapons as long as mankind inhabits this planet. There are other comparisons; Syria is even worse than Libya. This being part of the observation, how are we expecting to coerce North Korea; Iran; and future ones that are yet to surface, into refraining from building nuclear reactors and then to develop their own nuclear weapons? Because these and other countries, having taken ample notice of the Libyan invasion - which went way beyond the UN mandate of a No Fly Zone - will not now give up their plans for a nuclear deterrent.

Yet the No Fly Zone had been so effective, from so early on, that - in Libya - not one bird flew, let alone any aircraft. Mr Obama, you may have noticed, was rather reluctant to play a prominent part in that foray. Mr Cameron, on the other hand, in his staccato style and eager to propel himself onto the world stage - in the hope of enhancing his reputation as a world leader - went in gung-ho and gave his own interpretation as to what a no-fly zone means. Well not many people bought that. Most British people believe that it was all part of some unfinished business going back to what happened outside the Libyan embassy in London in 1984 when PC Yvonne Fletcher was murdered. And also for what has still not come to a satisfactory conclusion regarding the Lockerbie plane bombing. A whole load of divisiveness was part of that mission. Supporting rebels for regime change, in a way as blatant as we have done, can only result in us seeing, in the future, outsiders assisting terrorists in our own backyard.

For if we claim to have started on the moral high ground, why did we embark so glaringly with jingoism to effect regime change? We know that what we did was illegal and so does the British establishment; yet on numerous occasions those in Britain, who represent us, claim it was for our benefit. What benefits? We do not want them simply claiming that migrants would have come here because that would only have been the tail-end of the story. More likely it was to grease our economy with a few oil deals.

10 A DWINDLING POOL IN THE BOILING SUN

Now having muddied the waters of the world, what are we messing up for the future generations within our own society? Well, the system we currently have of sanctioning faith schools is certainly one very unpalatable cocktail. I say this because, in so doing, it is unwittingly creating enclaves within our cities that will cause history to haunt us for many decades to come.

And to think that we spent many years in combating apartheid in South Africa; and continue to do so wherever we find it raising its ugly head. Yet we now appear to have lost our focus; even though we have an ethos of equal opportunities and diversity. But in what way, you may ask, have we lost our focus? Well, it is by allowing children to go to segregated schools. Because these schools groom their pupils in the outdated beliefs of their own mired practices, which have been handed down by cultures that are irrelevant in today's social climate.

Therefore we can hardly expect these pupils - when they have made it into the mainstream of life -to be compliant in diversity and equal opportunities. Not, at any rate, when we have allowed them to be differentiated at such a tender age. After all, we can hardly expect them to have the flexibility of diversity and equal opportunities when they have grown up not having been predominately trained otherwise throughout their education. So to get them to change their mind-set as adults would indeed be a difficult task.

Yet not such a difficult task as trying, in some way, to control our growth in population.

It is pointless for any minister to go to the press, or use any media or TV, to give any prediction as to what the population will be by 2030. But here we are; a country of a small land capacity barely half the size of Germany; France or Spain with a population per square mile far exceeding any of those other countries. And with the British people, in terms of military might, who are no longer great because we haven't got the financial capacity now. For instance, we have only a skeleton army compared to what we had in the 60's and 70's. We've already talked about different types of conflict and different forms of battles. But even with little Libya we were buckling at the knees. Libya had open skies for us to saturate it with bombs, yet we had to go to the Americans to re-intensify the hardware over it. We needed US aid, even though we had the French alongside us doing the greater share of the assault. Despite all this, we were still creaking at the seams.

You see, when I speak, I speak as I see it and I do not think I see it wrongly. I have no political affiliation. I have only voted twice in my life. To me, it makes no difference who wins and who loses. Because sometimes, listening to them, there seems to be a difference of opinion. Some are talking about reducing numbers of Non-EU immigrants. Yet certain manufacturers say we need them. I am not disputing that. But if we need skilled workers can't we get them from the EU? I know we've got an agreement but we should be like the French and do what is in the best interest of the country. They are saying that there is no more room for any more immigrants. I think we are in that situation ourselves.

As I walk around the schools I see that there are lots of immigrant children. So what is going to happen in twenty years' time? Add to this that many of these people do not believe in contraception; they are indulging in population explosion. So, where we were once a mighty world power we are in steep decline. We have lost our industrial base - never to return to it. We know we need to make oil deals to grease our economy; but we still require much more before we can talk about growth. Not only in cash; we've got to halt the decline. Growth does not come when the decline is operational.

Other people will tell us that we are moving into a technological sphere. But what are they implying? That things are going to become brilliant? Maybe, but only for a selective few; and those will be predominately in the domain of the strong. On our present trajectory we are looking at a bastion of underprivileged who, since the demise of the industrial era, have been struggling much more than they were before the industrial revolution.

Technology does of course have benefits but it has its limits; because technology is accompanied by innovations which entail reductions in manpower. So what do we do with the reduction of man power? Where do they go? The pool of survival is rapidly dwindling. And even if we make an economic recovery, can any politician of any sincerity tell us what percentage of the population will be the beneficiaries? Well I can tell you it will be a minority not a majority. Also, any work we have here is being outsourced to other countries. And this has become the norm; constantly seeking a ready source of cheap labour.

The labour force which we have here cannot possibly compete in the world market, especially as our economy is a very highly taxed one. Yet our raw material, which for decades we were able to acquire upon the cheap, is no longer cheap. We have to pay much more and I am afraid that it is going to continue to be that way. Countries that have not yet emerged on the horizon will soon be springing up; it is only a matter of time. So the dash to prop up the economy will become even more competitive than what it is now, which means that - with the steep population rise - we will be struggling on the economic side.

Now, it seems to be believed by some politicians that we are at the forefront of the Green Environment. We should stop being reactive in our thinking. Proactive can usually be a plus. If we believe that we are going to be leaders in this field then we are absolutely day-dreaming. Other countries in the world are catching up with us in technology; even when we are the creators or inventors they will soon catch up to the point where we will lose that monopoly. So, basically, we are finding ourselves in a pool of water beneath the boiling sun in a dwindling pool.

Would any politician be prepared to tell us, with any authenticity, how they anticipate managing the population increase which we are definitely going to have? Because having lost our position as world leaders and no longer able to dominate in any particular field, our own people - prior even to the prevailing recession - were struggling with the housing situation. And even if that improved we would also require more medical practitioners of various categories. So how are these consultants, surgeons, GPS, nurses, etc, going to be funded? Where is the revenue going to come from? These are serious questions because we are looking at improvements in four or five years' time.

But when it improves, to what levels will it improve? Who will be the beneficiaries -the shareholders? So will they be more flexible and give more to the workers? I don't think so, bearing in mind the economic factors which are very dire at present. Even in 2010, workers in the construction industry were earning far less than they were at the turn of the century. So unless we embark on a new type of revolution; economic ethos, redistribution not simply of wealth but of opportunities, they will only get worse. Take small businesses for example. They have long been regarded as vital to our country's economy, yet now they are being squeezed out by conglomerates or the bigger establishments. And with these leviathans seeking always to become bigger, larger, and more powerful, how will small businesses grow?

All the time we see family owned ventures being trampled down by the power of the mighty. Along our high streets small businesses open where, prior to that, there were dead ones. But they are only replacing what was previously in existence. Within the distance of a few hundred metres, you will come to observe a multitude of duplicates; all cutting each other's throats. Not intentionally, but out of sheer desperation to find the oxygen for survival. And they are forever in a losing battle because as the mighty grow mightier, the weak grow weaker. The strong therefore grow mighty at the demise of the weak. And the weak ones have no means of escape. Our fathers, who were the lifeblood of our countryside, are finding it increasingly more difficult to earn a living out of their slave labour. And in so doing, it creates a chain reaction on the rest of our community. Even though, during the final forty years of the 20th Century, mankind had made huge scientific and technological advances to the benefit of the human race.

Yet any administration or establishment which finds itself embarking on projects or issues of serious national concern, that are dictated by circumstances and not the consequences of sound judgement, are never-the-less displaying all the hallmarks of decline. Because, having achieved the bracket of supremacy for many decades it is now becoming increasingly difficult for Britain to sustain the performance required to maintain this once dominant position. We are not blessed with mineral wealth. Our industrial base is all but gone. This is reality; the moment of truth. It is, therefore, the task of all those in responsible positions to dispel the gloom; to inspire and rally their subordinates.

Now, while optimism is an essential element, superficiality is not an option. Countries that were proudly basking and reaping the rewards of the industrial revolution are now relying more heavily on the shifting sands of banking and the cajoling promise of export. So, circumstances have come to dictate to us that the word, "Growth" is hugely important to our survival. But when we use the word "Growth," in what shape or form? The small businesses - those, that is, that still survive - how will they compete and in what market? Our manufacturing base has gone. The industrial revolution, which started with a bang, went with a whimper. The shipyards used to flourish. The motor industry used to do exceedingly well. Our machinery used to be manufactured in places like the Midlands and exported the world over. Yet all these have now been decimated. We have come to the point where we are outsourcing much of our work to foreign lands when we badly need the employment for our own.

But if government departments, claiming for the purpose of cost cutting, are outsourcing their work to foreign countries then what next? We have seen Birmingham City Council outsourcing one hundred jobs. For all we know this might be the forerunner of things to come. If we take what they say at face value, which is that it's for the purpose of cost-cutting, then taking this figure - that's one hundred people put out of work for cost cutting. What happened to these people? How will they survive? Will the government assist them? Will they be getting benefit and will they have the same spending power as when they were employed? So, would such forced unemployment be of benefit to the economy at large?

Well, even if it was, we have to visualize beyond that. It's not only the pounds and pence in the pockets, or the purses, of those people laid off- but also the message that permeates from one generation to the next. This means that the nightmare scenario; the disenchantment; the destabilizing of the family unit is passing from the parents to their children. So in evaluating the cost of that we can hardly claim that it is for cost-cutting purposes because outsourcing this work, to save costs, harms the family circle and that is of far more value than what we receive by out-sourcing.

I don't need to spell this out. I'm taking you on a journey and you can see along the line.

It's like you say to your children, "Next year we'll go on holiday," and then suddenly you say to them, "We can't go - Daddy's out of work." That's not going to be happy reading on their features. The younger ones were probably looking forward to it. It is very demoralising for you to see this. Just imagine you're a council worker and your job's just gone to India.

You're likely to be "F'ing and Blinding" at home about, 'They're taking our jobs.' Well, you don't mean it in that context but your teenagers pick up on it. They get the wrong idea. But you've got to have sympathy with them. It's hard to keep them on the straight and narrow when they see their spending power disappear overnight, which is having an untold amount of damage;

you can't place a value on it. Even the Treasury is losing out on lost tax. Yet you can't afford to take your clothes to the dry cleaners or take the kids out for the day. It's more than just the monetary terms we have to look at here. It's our whole way of life that is being threatened.

11 THE ABYSS BELOW

So when we talk in terms about a revolution we have to think in terms of something new; something which is sustainable. We need to learn from past experience. Remember; the industrial age came and it only lasted for so long. Now we've moved into the Technological Age with its benefits to mankind in the field of medicine and economic purposes but only to the minority, not to the majority.

We have seen in the last few decades a growth in millionaires and more recently a growth in billionaires; but we have also seen a growth in the underprivileged. And there are many on the north side of the divide, and many more on the equator - that's the imaginary line mid-way between rich and poor - they're probably looking at the abyss down below. Why? Because they are sliding down obviously - sliding down into the nightmare of the "Green Environment."

That's because no one has ever come on TV or in the press to tell us how many people will, at its peak, be employed. Or should we expect even this? We talk about electric cars; but how many people are going to be employed? Technology moves at a very fast pace from one country to the next. Nothing is really safe. We've come to learn that. Remember the damage caused to Fukushima Daiichi, Japan when an earthquake generated tsunami swamped the nuclear facility there. But it's not just natural disasters. We've come to learn that computers are not safe. We've come to learn that a lot of the people who work within our system are not necessary reliable.

Besides, the technology can move from one country to the next in very rapid time. We're not really going to steal a march to the point where we can benefit by more than a decade or two. We might be able get new products out first, but by how much and for how long can we maintain such a lead? Not only that, but a lot of money would have gone into research - how much will we be able to recoup of this cost? Others will soon be on our backs stealing our own ingenuity.

They've been talking about the "Green Environment" long enough now. Yet there is a conflict with the "Green Environment." We must bear in mind, right at our elbow, is technology; innovation; and these are also going to be part and parcel of the "Green Environment." So while our captains of industry boast about, "Achieving certain objectives by creating," what do we do with the scrap-heap of human beings? Because the vast number of human beings then will not be compatible with the development of technology.

I mean, we hear about three hundred million pounds profit being made in a quarter by one particular supermarket giant. But when you're there you see new faces. It tells you the staff turn-over is high. So you know the wages they're being paid is very meagre. And they're mostly part-time. Now, this probably suits some people, but most only work part-time because they cannot get full-time. Yet it's not possible to support a family on those wages. That's why we need a new type of revolution. We've had the industrial one and now we've got the technological one. But this age, the consumers are letting the bosses make all the money. Maybe the consumers are happy to spend the little money they have. But do we really need so much? Some of us have two mobile phones. Since mobile phones have come our way, some of us can't walk down the road without talking to people all over the world. But we still have to pay for it, which means that the phone companies are making hundreds of millions of pounds profits.

So those unfortunate enough to be south of the divide are being kept there. Some appear to be happy about this; they are the ones who keep dreaming and fantasizing - but in reality there's no light at the end of the tunnel for them. Because that depends on growth; and this leaves me with a sort of bewilderment. Is it, I wonder, out of aspiration, knowledge, optimism or duty?

Now I feel that, if it is out of aspiration, then the rich and poor share that same ideal. If it is knowledge; we would like the politicians to give us a clearer idea how it is going to come about. If it is optimism, is it also tempered with pessimism because we are at the crossroads; confronted with reality. If it is duty; then should that duty be sincere or ambiguous or might it even be a false promise? For if we say, "We have aspiration," then even

61

with knowledge, optimism and duty, it still leaves us facing an overwhelming challenge. Because in all this we find ourselves relying very much on an over-loaded truck, which may very easily overbalance.

Now, if this hoped for growth is coming through the banking sector, I wonder just how volatile this is going to be. Gone are the days when we had Mr Alan Greenspan of the US Treasury Department. When he was about to take action; either to increase or lower interest rates, the entire western world and many of the emerging economical nations were waiting with bated breath. Now the entire concept has changed and is still changing. We have to be very outspoken in explaining our real position amongst the family of nations because we are a declining force. There are many aspects of our economy that are palpably clear for all to see.

On the other hand we've got emerging countries, like the Chinese, who have stolen a march on the western powers. They have moved into Africa with great dexterity, cornering the resources there, which is depriving us of what we would have probably liked to do. We have, for a long time, watched from the side-lines without apparently giving a thought concerning the Chinese adventure on the African continent. Yet we seem to believe that we are still at the cutting edge of technology. Well, we may very well be leading many nations in that particular field. But then it must be realised that we've spent an enormous amount on research before ever getting onto the production line.

So while we can joyfully say, "Britain is a market leader," there is not enough light to adequately illuminate the dark areas of our faltering economy. Our kids are growing up in this environment. They hear how things use to be and they compare it with what they see now. But who will speak up for them? No one! No one in Leadership speaks up for the underprivileged. Well, as long as no one speaks or is able to take effective action for the underprivileged they will keep on creating an underclass. And this will always be a thorn in the flesh because when they become parents, then their off-springs; they will be the off-springs of the environment that has created them. These people will always have a plethora of sympathisers.

So you see, people talk about the economy being like this or like that; but how many people really notice things like 1.4 or 1.5 percent? Those on the bottom rung of the ladder don't. They just hear this as a number or a figure. They do not feel it in their pockets. It is no good some government financial institution coming out with this sort of talk when the people don't experience this for themselves. It is like being on the outside looking in. Now until this can put this right much more vociferously than just mere talking and, unless we are truly championing the cause of the underprivileged, we are just empty windbags.

Now, we keep on hearing new ideas, but new ideas are irrelevant if not supported by substance because people are looking forward eagerly in their desire to believe in them.

However, when nothing materialises it leaves people even more dismayed than before these words were mooted. Because people do have high expectations and they are fully justified in this. I have heard it said, in the past, of the general public indulging in the culture of envy, but it would make a welcome change for any minister, or one that aspires to be so, to see them castigate some of the tabloids for brandishing celebrities on their front pages repeatedly to excess. It creates a culture of envy when we see the privileges of wealth so well documented.

But rather than all this sensationalism, the front pages of our newspapers should contain news relating to the economy, or the prime minister or the government, or portray someone that has done something good. Yet they just keep filling these pages repeatedly with some highly overpaid individual, for just kicking a football. Not only that, but the same story often crops up in one form or another for a whole week in one paper or another. The front page ought to the preserve of serious news; like the state of the nation and inspiring people to work hard.

And because of this you now get young people not wanting to do an apprenticeship or even study too hard when they go to university. Those that want to succeed these days are very few indeed. Just look at the premier division. How many of our players can you say are world class? I mean, David Beckham was good at crossing the ball over into the box. Yet at international level he never got a look in. He was just an average footballer. If he was world class he could bypass his opponent. It's the same with African-Caribbean youngsters. It's about time they woke up. They are not doing nearly anywhere near enough. I can say this. I have been proactive. I sincerely wish that lots of ministers and people in responsible position, while they may not echo total agreement with what is written and read, would read this. It would be to them very much an eye opener. I am not alone with these beliefs and I am proud to state that I am sufficiently tenacious and disciplined, with honest and indomitable courage, to put pen to paper.

Out of what is written, I sincerely challenge any to give me the time to sit in front of the cameras with them to debate these subjects. Surprise, surprise, we would, for the national audience, seek an electronic vote and lay our credibility on the line. Now, I'm not prepared to sit in judgement on one single politician. Such judgement should be the preserve of the British people. There was a television programme recently with Kelvin McKenzie and Jack Straw on it. I can't understand why people think that everything has to be so taboo. They won't talk about it even if it's true. But Jack Straw did. I would like to go cap in hand to him and extend a welcoming hand to him for his bravery. I feel it's about time for someone who belongs to the upper echelons of British Society to speak with total honesty. Jack Straw wasn't talking about "Left Wing" or "Right Wing" agendas. What he said, lots of people know about. I know about it. Well I find it exasperating that whenever they have people on television or they want to publicize something, they bring in people with well-known faces. But that doesn't mean that they know about the particular issue at hand. Often what they say is not appropriate.

So that's why I welcome Jack Straw's comments. So often, when they get people on TV, they get the wrong people. You don't get people from the Silent Majority. You get people who are looked on as a cut-above the ordinary people. It's like a certain politician that I see shopping sometimes. This person once was a local member of parliament; but you never saw this person communicating with anyone. They don't talk to people like you and me.

So where do these people get their ideas from? Even though they are supposed to represent us you never see them come down here to listen to the people. Yet some of these people were once students and they might by intelligent, but to be really able then you must be able to operate in many different orbits. Then you will have an advantage over other people.

And you can tell those people who have this advantage by their body language. A trained man could tell these people quickly, like a trained detective can spot the sort of person someone is. I'm like that. When I meet someone for the first time I get an idea what they are like within the first few seconds. I can read a lot into their body language, and I can identify their profile. This is not something I've been trained in. It's a matter of experience. And then, when I notice what a person is like, I adapt to that person. If I notice that they have a good profile, then I give them a lot of attention. Others, I just make sure that I don't offend them; however, I may not have much to do with them after that.

12 THE REALMS OF POVERTY

These days I feel that we have a shortage of quality politicians. To me there is nothing outstanding on the horizon; at least not on this side of the world. I think that Obama is not too bad because he is trying to build bridges. We are much closer to the Russians now then since 1945. But our prime minister is ambitious; he has to be careful. He's being a bit 'gung-ho' over the other politicians. In retrospect he looks a bit too 'Russian'; pushing too much for his own corner. However, if he demonstrated greater political aplomb, he could achieve much more.

You see you can't go around acting like you're the greatest. Now Cassius Clay claimed to be the greatest; but then he went and proved it. But you have to prove it, and you may not prove it. David Cameron may have had some outstanding successes, but if you give yourself away through your body language then other people will go out of their way to frustrate you.

Take, for example, the attempt to secure the 2018 World Cup. Now, David Cameron went and he was very prominent. Yet he was very circumspect. He brought Prince William, he brought David Beckham. Well, this is over the top. Just because he brought Prince William doesn't necessarily make David Cameron look any better. By doing this you could be showing too much of your hand. Then people will go out of their way to frustrate what you are doing. Sometimes, you know, 'less is best'.

Remember we were once a great nation. We had a great empire; although now we are in rapid decline. Hopefully we won't end up at the bottom, but we are certainly nowhere near the top. What will keep us afloat longer is the manner that we market democracy. That will keep us in their good books for longer. Yet there are always those that will criticize you, but not openly. Except for the Chinese; they don't want to hear about democracy.

Once, we used to be part of the "Four Powers". That was the United States, France, Britain and Russia. Then we became part of the G8 and now we are part of the G20. You see we are no longer aloft. China never used to be part of it but now we need to keep in with the Chinese for our very survival. This is because the world is being taken apart - bit by bit - in a gradual manner. There are many countries who aspire to rise above the clouds. But it is getting chronic. Sooner or later no one will be able to live in salubrious surroundings or enjoy their desired opulence.

We only have to look at our motor industry. As competition increases, car manufacturers are being forced into mergers. It's got nothing to do with their performance or marketing. Our politicians should tell people the real truth. We cannot even afford a sizable army because we do not possess the financial resources. Yet such a thing was unthinkable in the immediate post-war period. No one then would, for a minute, suggest that we merge any part of our armed forces with any of our European partners but the fact that we have taken that step with our nearest continental neighbour indicates that we are on the remorseless slide down the pecking order.

In so doing, we are following the pattern of many other nations. Large ones even; where too many have been allowed in, to the detriment of those deprived. And such deprivation is reflected in the larger arena of society. When you go along, it is truly evident that there are many people in our society who are not lazy. However, because of being deprived, it is their kids who are the ones that populate the penal establishments. We know that there are some in prison who belong to the upper class but they are in the minority. These ones tend to be involved in fraud, yet their sentences are light compared to the finance involved.

Therefore we need to have a complete revamp of society; no matter how difficult it may be. This has to be done if we are to redress the imbalance, because - as mentioned earlier - it is all too easy for some people to get excessive amounts of cash and returns on their investments. This money must be coming from somewhere and some of us must be paying it at a price. And this price is our existence and our future. It does not inspire us to be hard working, decent and honest. Yet it's not as though we are working any less hard than some people who are worth billions and billions. It should be defined; to have a better spread of wealth. Getting more people to play a part as long as their health permits; whatever they are able to contribute to society and still earn an acceptable living for their output.

We know there are people who claim long-term illness. Well, stringent examination should be the order of the day. And when they are found to be able to do something to contribute to society they should be ordered, in a very firm yet reasonable manner, to earn their keep. It is not exactly a pleasant idea that some people go to work on a daily basis and part of their hard-earned cash has to go to people moving around and playing high and mighty and giving themselves the air of confidence - as if they are geniuses living in our society - without breaking into a sweat.

The Riot Act should be read to everyone; come what may. If they are genuinely ill, they should be assisted. But if not; there should be no words minced. They should go out to work. But the return should reflect the effort. People shouldn't live in a society that has so many structures where unpleasant and hard work has come to be regarded as the cheapest earners. And although many of our high earners would disagree - it is totally wrong that someone who is out sweeping the streets in all weathers and getting pneumonia and such like is getting the lowest pay. This isn't right. Okay, no one wants to do this work - it's like being punished. But give these people their due - they are prepared to do this rather than commit crime, and then be incarcerated and live off the state. They are prepared to get up at six in the morning, going out picking up litter bins and we don't even give them the time of day. But why should their wages be lower than someone who just goes and sits in an office? It isn't right.

As it is, for all our delusions, we are relentlessly moving into the realms of poverty.

While a lot of our inhabitants do not want to make such an open admission, their dire straits of life have already led them well into this bracket. It may look like we are doing well when we see lots of people taking to the airways. But these seasonal flights abroad conceal an underlying trend. That is, that there are tens of thousands of people who cannot afford to take a holiday away from the shores of the United Kingdom.

And statistics in themselves do not reveal this trend because the government manufactures statistics that are too inept. They do not give the complete breakdown of the so called, "Broken Society." The prime minister himself dubbed the phrase, "Broken Society" but, instead of using this phrase, he should have looked at it in its realism. Poverty is rife; and the misdeeds that we see in the everyday lives of those caught in its trap are very much so because of the state of their lives. Within their own limits, they see no other way and they are very much like man-eating animals by virtue of this being the only existence known to them. So, eating you up is, to them, a ready source of existence.

Not only that, but we have also entered an era where there is talk about "banding" I see this as a form of making people, who are currently in a job of work, take a reduction in salary. So; more work - less pay. But although the government have claimed to have taken austerity measures to rebalance the economy, what are they actually promising us? Is it that the economy will be balanced and people will again receive their dues? If so, who is going to decide the pay structure? Who will ensure that we are paid correctly for the duties that we are required to perform?

Does this give rise for concern? We have reached a defining moment, like when the conductor on the bus says to the passengers, "All change please!" But in our case, the ones confined, there is no "please" about it. Not that we were going to be pleased anyway, so "please" is too subtle to be used on us. For good measure we are, and I stick my neck out at this moment of writing, being forced to change to the lower step. But then, we have declined immensely and we have been fighting to stay afloat. Some may cling on a while, but the trend is one way; probably for many generations to come. Maybe forever.

And, to top it all, we still have more people from the mainland to come; even though we cannot deal adequately with those we have now. So much for the promised reduction of class sizes in our schools. How much longer do we have to go before seeing significant reductions? The answer lies right here. Anyone who wants to repudiate those challenges placed before their very eyes - they need to answer these questions convincingly and honestly. Now we are having a gathering storm of children, piling up like pyramids, unable to find classes to be at school.

Yet with no programme of school building it can only get worse. But even should we want to embark on such a programme, how is it going to be funded? What is going to be the end result? It just shows how much we have become a declining force even within the last fifty years. And that's not the only example. We once had factories producing clothes in Whitechapel; Greeks, Turks - lots of different people working in them. But now we've allowed just a few big companies to own most of the retail outlets. Look at the petrol stations: nearly all are now owned by Asda, Tesco or Sainsbury's - everywhere you go; it's just these you see. The ordinary person has no space to manoeuvre. People are being shunted into a corner and once they are in that corner it becomes more difficult for them to get out of it. Life for us is becoming hopeless. And people are more reluctant to strike than they were ten years ago. We've seen it with the bus drivers - they have been forced to take a wages cut. Well, that doesn't make for a good working force.

Now, we were promised that the NHS was safe. Yet the waiting list is rising. But we are told, "It doesn't matter that the waiting list is rising; it's the service which is provided that matters." Well, when are we going to stop listening to this sort of garbage that is being directed to our ears? When one set of politicians were in opposition they were criticising the government for hospitals having long waiting lists. However, now that they are in power they are saying that the numbers do not matter - it's the care that's important.

And another thing; we've now got to the disgraceful point where we do not have aircraft carriers any more. Even seeking to build two; it is now expected that only one will enter service and that is many years away. But for all we know, within another few short years, there might be a decision taken to defer even that one from entering service. Assuming it gets to completion. So, if we have to live within our means - fair enough - but our leaders should first of all be looking after the people who elect them to power. We shouldn't be moving around, seeking to be the Policeman of the World, or seeking to consistently be giving welcome to others rather than looking after our own. This oversaturation has put us all in the same boat - whether nationals or visitors - we will not gather strength; we will all be weak. Not strong enough to lift up the weaker ones and also not strong enough to stay within reasonable strength.

Now those people who look at the wider Europe and claim they pay taxes.

Is it not time we stopped to think how much they get out of us? Because we are less rich; we are getting poorer by the day. And no matter how much we try to rely on modern technology, we still have to do something revolutionary, in fact; go full-circle. Do what the Chinese did; go to other countries and help them to redevelop like we did in the heady days of the Empire. But this time not to colonize - but to assist. We do not have the land mass for the population that we are likely to have in another thirty or forty years from now. This system of diversity it is good in one way but we still have to exam it closely. Many of the foreign nationals coming here do not face the problems that British workers have to put up with. We have to fill in forms of application to acquire jobs and we are forced to accept contracts which are legally binding. The idea of being diverse and having equal opportunities should be applied right across the board. We are becoming a laughing stock. We should take note; have certain covert actions to investigate whether other groups are executing their work fairly. It would be interesting to see just how diverse they are.

The system seems designed to get British workers to have both feet in one shoe. That is not really fair; it is grossly unfair. So now, the British people are confined to lower wages and being demanded to produce more. This is economic blackmail at its worse. It does not make for a motivated work force. There are lots of people who are just on the brink of poverty. Now, poverty is staring them in the face and as much as they do not want to openly admit it -they are right now within its embrace. The future for them, and their children, is rather bleak.

We are now entering another challenge. We look at the United States; phasing out its re-useable craft. They can no longer afford such extravagant exploits and it is only a matter of time before the Russians follow suit. How long can they sustain sending out American astronauts or putting space material into docking stations?

They may go for another few more short years, but the time is limited. All the nations of the world are facing growing challenges. Mankind had better step off its high horse, believing that we are infallible. The challenges are glaring; weather patterns and weather conditions are hugely unpredictable. The resources which we relied on for our existence are getting more and more difficult to obtain. Decisions as to which fuel to use for our services are now are no longer fluent. There is a huge debate about to unfold as to what should be done. Even when decisions are arrived at, they are not arrived at with great confidence. But now it's decision time. Mankind is beginning to be like trapped rats in a cage. We are experiencing severe droughts; more volcanic eruptions; more frequent tsunamis -the fuel resources are diminishing. Even the coal has become more difficult and expensive to extract.

We are, it seems, caught in limbo. Should we go nuclear for our energy and risk people's indignation? We certainly cannot embark on such a programme with total confidence in technology. We have seen appalling catastrophes from Bhopal to the recent Japanese disaster. Can many nations, for example, afford the preventative measures needed to avert nuclear dangers? Can we see the magnitude of these nuclear dangers? Can we guarantee that we going to be bomb-proof? And these are not the only dangers; how - for example - do we deal with spent fuel rods?

It is still highly debatable, on the universal front, how we are going to get the fuel and energy which we require. We are seeking to explore more of the ocean; more of the land, but there are limitations. Even in so doing, we sometimes have to breach nature. In the food we consume, for instance, we are having problems. It has been forced upon us to eat GM food. But are the masses convinced of its safety? Even if we get answers, they can hardly assure us that we are safe from any effects because we are dealing with chemicals and tampering with nature. We must always be aware - nature is the supreme master. Whatever we do, how long we do it for - it is like a pugilist in the ring for the 15-round contest. No matter how much you are winning on points at the moment; nature will emerge victorious in the end. It cannot be defeated.

However, if we look at a lot of our leaders; can they be challenged about their ideals and their promises? Whatever they say, it is looking less compact; thinner and thinner; less convincing; less credible. We need people who can tell us what the next phase is going to be; not what is before our very eyes -it is not sustainable. Within our own sphere we have to seek a better present; a better tomorrow. We need to ensure that our future generations are educated in a manner to better prepare them for the challenges which will confront them.

Our funds, which they claim can do the many things we're promised, are very much in jeopardy. The recovery that some claim will happen - we would like to know when it is likely to begin. Those we elect do not give us great confidence. We only hope for the future, because we cannot obliterate history. This is our yardstick. We have been through the industrial age; we have been through the atomic age and we are now in the technological age. We know, undoubtedly, that mankind is living rather longer but at the same time the world is growing hungrier. And this is as of right now - not simply for the future - but as of now.

But if the world is growing that much hungrier, why have we not solved that in the last 30 - 40 years? It is precisely like taking medication and having an over-dose. At all times, when we go to college; when we go to university or other faculties of learning, we are hell-bent on finding how to produce what we produce easier and quicker. Yet as we do this on one side; we are oblivious to the human element that is necessary for mankind's survival. This means, in actual fact, that we are unwittingly squeezing the human race simply for our own survival.

Will we come to our senses when we find the world is on the move and not only in the Middle East? Will we be finding, as the pattern of things to come, that as people grow more uncomfortable looking at the riches of the rich that it will be difficult to live in complete freedom? Then every step you take in freedom will be a perilous journey. Because, with all the goods you want to parade, there will be other people who, by needs of wanting a better living, develop envy. So with all the luxury and the artifacts you have stored up in the home, you will have to be guarded by electronic surveillance; high electrified fences and maybe guard dogs. It will be difficult to parade jewellery in populated places.

Therefore, what is the point of having riches to excess if it cannot be enjoyed in the manner in which it was intended to? You will have unwittingly become your own prisoner.

There is nothing one can do in order to preach morality to any when the world gets to this stage; it is a case of life or death, a case of need.

Unpalatable as it is - it is a case of necessity and we know that necessity is the mother of invention. Which means that people will lose their morals just in search of their own ideal and that ideal, without a doubt, is survival.

13 DISCIPLINE AND THE STRUCTURE OF SOCIETY

Well, the future may seem bleak, but that doesn't mean that we cannot at least try to turn things around. As I mentioned earlier, I do not see the world as a dull place. I enjoy meeting people and, because I have always taken an interest in what is going on around me, I am never at a loss for words. I used to meet up with an old fellow named Jim. Jim used to live near me by Victoria Park. But now he lives in Romford. He liked to sit on a park bench and if I saw him I would talk to him. He used to be a Black Cab driver years ago, but before that he was an amateur boxer. So we often talked about boxing. Then, one day, while we were talking he was astonished to hear that I knew about some of the old boxers who were around in the 1920's and 30's. That was because I used to read about them. He used to enjoy our little talks.

Anyway, during the time that I have been here I have also noticed that there are organisations which seek to protect civil liberties and promote human rights. Now whilst such organisations do have some valid points within the defence of the various concerns they propagate, it is only right that checks and balances be put in place. Such accountability is long overdue because the scale has tipped excessively in favour of these organisations.

So one-sided has it now become that we experience the malaise of their doctrine in the twisting and turning; ducking and diving culture of, "Who should we blame'?" The system and establishment have to share a great deal of responsibility for this. I do not accept that, when youngsters are moving along the wrong path, they, "Should be allowed complete freedom to proceed." Little wonder then that professional teachers from abroad, when they come over here for a period to teach, very often quit in utter disgust and return prematurely to their homeland. Now don't get me wrong, there are some beautiful kids - but there is also a deft shortage of obedience. A word or phrase which is ever hardly put to these kids during their development is that, "Obedience is a necessity!" Yet it is common knowledge that the system requests the youngsters to report their parents should they receive any form of firm discipline from them. It is very fortunate when some parents experience their kids growing without such needs. But when they request the need for correction without a deterrent it soon becomes a very un-holy alliance not only within the family circle but also in the community at large.

This is very often, undoubtedly, the product of the system. But the system and the establishment are forever in denial to acknowledge their responsibility in failing to get it right at the initial stages. When kids know that their parents are the authority, do we know the parents' wishes? It is always the risky road to use that freedom and convert it to abuse and very often society in general pays a very high price for the wrong decisions taken. Yet unfortunately parents are left with no recourse or any form of sanction, even as a deterrent. There are plenty of very good parents in the land. However, they are very much aware that they run the very high risk of criminalisation.

Therefore the kids run amok which retards their education. They become unruly, laughing at discipline and taking everything for granted. Yet we find that the government simply passes the buck onto parents and teachers. It is like placing vast amounts of police on the beat with their hands tied behind their backs. Their effectiveness is of course inhibited. In the same way the battles between the rising generations are lost, not necessarily in the late stages of life, but because the system becomes vanquished from a very early age. But whenever the government review these issues it is never revealed how they have delegated power to our youngsters. No, instead they shift the blame onto parents and teachers. Well, you can see that the system really deserves a fair share of the blame.

And then the government go on about, "Short; sharp treatment" when these kids reach 14, 15 or 16 years of age. They apply this by putting them in correction centres. But this is no solution. Very often they come out worse than before. Because putting them together in such an environment - with like-minded individuals - and with no one to control them, encourages them to brag about their exploits. Therefore they do no more than inspire waywardness. So the system needs to put its own house in order.

Discipline has its virtues in the structure of society. It helps people to have a greater awareness of their own self and those around them. It also helps them to be more aware of what's going on and boosts their development; shifting from stagnation and journeying into progression. It creates a positive attitude which helps them to develop ethics, dignity, integrity and a respect for themselves and others. This is better for the economy as a whole and better for their own families at large. Therefore, rather than telling kids to report on their parents, the government should foster an attitude in these children of obedience to seniors; be it mum and dad or the teachers in the classroom.

We know there are instances of abuse, ministers can therefore suggest, "Make it a legal requirement that wherever a kid comes to be registered, then whoever is in a responsible position to do so, issue a small handout - not to much reading; making it clear and concise as to the do's and don'ts; what is acceptable and, within limits, what is and is not and what would be the justice should they transgress," but with the kids being aware of the deterrent.

Co-existence, throughout the family life, brings greater reward to the family at large and also the establishment's penal reform because it is very likely that fewer youngsters will have to be placed in detention centres or be put into homes. We know, from experience, that whenever groups of youngsters are clustered together in an uncontrollable environment that this promises a highly toxic cocktail.

As it is, we are now in dire straits. We have people producing in this country whose progression and ethics are virtually zero. Should they be allow to develop as they are now then image; by 2020, how many more will be incarcerated? Therefore, by failing to embark on a variation of education of some groups, irrespective of dissenting voices from so-called community leaders, the truth has to be confronted head on. Should they want to put up a veneer in defence they should be questioned as to what the solution should be. To keep on travelling on this particular path is too hazardous to proceed.

There are virtues in educating them by using psychology. They have to realise that they must change their ways. Yet to target only a certain like-minded group as a quick-fix solution is not the answer. Such deception is dangerous. We very often talk about "Stop and Search." Sometimes it may be unjustified but often it is. When we talk about proportionate and disproportionate policing then voices within the community are quick to claim certain groups are disproportionately stopped and searched. This may well be correct but are we always to be A guided by statistics?

I have grave doubts that we should always go by statistics. Should we put our name on the chopping block; that statistics should be the guiding principle? Well, there is a yard-stick which is not openly spoken of. Looking within London itself, looking at the number of teenage fatalities - can the propagators of statistics give an explanation? Well, we all know who comes top of the list of teenage fatalities.

We should stop bandying about what is disproportionate and what is proportionate. If you are going to talk about what is proportionate then we want to look at the misdeeds being done by the group that comes top of the pile in violence which results in fatalities; shattering the lives of parents: mums and dads; brothers and sisters or their closed communities. This is a blight on the group itself. People view them with deep suspicion because they are seen very much as having this as a trade mark.

Yet there are many of us that don't like this. But we should be disciplining our children from a very early age - not treating them with kid gloves. When you tell them that they have to be in by nine 'o'clock at night then they should be in by that time. Not just going about like some of them do; they don't even know the time. They are out at ten or eleven at night. They tell you that they have been out with their friends, but they were probably outside a club - nowhere near where they tell you they've been. And they don't do their homework and so forth. A lot of the parents have problems getting their children to do their homework. When they try to tell them to do their homework the kids say, "No," because they know there is nothing you can do about it. Because the system says that parents cannot touch them. The system is not interested in whether the children are in default or if they are misbehaving. And the children know this. They are taught from an early age to report their parents to their teachers. Then the system comes down hard on the parents; wanting to know, "Have you touched them?" And if you have -then this is condemned as a "Criminal act." So the parents can do nothing because the system is against them.

Now, we are in a season of austerity and if we cannot get those youngsters to buck up their ideas then we are going to see much more homelessness from that particular group. It won't be long, because we have come to see what the pattern of life is shaping to. There are high earners - but those will stay that way, while those that aspire to do a hard day's work will find it more difficult to move up the ladder, unless they have their own business.

To do this though, they will have to be disciplined and committed if they hope to achieve success.

Now there are numerous clichés about the African-Caribbean community and in many cases those in that group do not seem to give due attention to what these clichés imply. They very often use the word, "Safe," they very often use the words, "Halle Selassie I." They claim to have culture. Every group, I believe, should have an identifiable culture. But when this no longer lines up with everyday life, in a different environment, some of what is claimed to be culture is no more than recently acquired habits. And even if it is something dating back centuries, they should not all be regarded as ideal in today's world. Just to give an example; there are still people on this planet who are prepared to take the life of some minor. This is supposed to be part of their culture; to engage in such rituals. Should anyone be claiming that this is culture and it should be embraced for dear life? I very much doubt it. Should the answer to that question be "Yes," then it should be jettisoned or put into the incinerator.

When we embark on burning ganja, idling about, saying, "Nothing is going on," then probably passing a spliff to each other to inhale, we are simply craving security. We want the easy enjoyment from it rather than engaging each other in positive thinking. We fool ourselves into thinking that we have found the ideal friends by mixing with like-minded people; hanging around and watching the world pass by. Such fantasising; imagining, but without concrete planning, is no more than living on a wave of wishful thinking.

When I look at the African-Caribbean community in the United Kingdom, I see that there are many decent people within it. There are some enterprising, but they are a small minority. Yet I find they are not honest enough to speak their own mind - how they see it, what they believe. Are they too apprehensive about antagonising the negative ones? Myself, a born African-Caribbean who came to the United Kingdom as a young person in the early 1960's, will not profess to say everything is excellent but the percentage of excellence is extremely high. I admit there's a lot of "Do-gooders" in Britain. Still, they do have a lot of patience and they do demonstrate a great deal of civility.

Of course there are prisons; of course there are convicts, of course there are bad-minded people - but you will get that in every land. However, just looking at the percentage of young African-Caribbean's who make up the prison population appals me. These young people do not appear to have any regard for the lives of others. But I am also disgusted at those adults, that I speak to, who hide behind the shield of what happened centuries ago.

Now I don't envisage anyone who has read the history of those times ever forgetting because it is within the archives of our own knowledge. But we have to be realistic; shake off the cobwebs of ineptitude and allow them to be blown into the wind. We must make a concerted effort to be more vocal, provided that we are truthful, and let our young people known that this is not the time to lay back and wallow in the past.

Neither should they take on the offence of others. Why do so many black boys here use American convicts as role models? It just shows how far they need to go before the young African-Caribbean community as a whole is recognised as being sufficiently high on the ladder of social acceptance. They should not wait for other groups to tell them; it should start within themselves. So don't be too patronising; this can do the community great damage and a continued disservice. Words must not be mixed; time is running out for them. As the world moves on, they are finding themselves further adrift.

Now what we should see - when we go to certain areas such as Southall or we go to Green Street in east London, or Brick Lane or Ilford or anywhere else - is shining examples for the youth of today; those - that is - who have survived the brutality of their own peers to be the men of tomorrow. Yet could we, by asking them politely, get frank answers from them? How do they equate to this comparison? What are their opinions? Have they got any excuses or doctrines as to what should be done? But I doubt that without appropriate role models there will be much hope for them.

14 THE LIGHT OF REDEMPTION

Today you will find that in the faculties of learning, when an Indian student seeks to expand his knowledge or her knowledge, they tend to be very businesslike. At a glance, it is not difficult to see their commitment to the objective. Unlike our African-Caribbean's, where there is a lot of play, a lot of game; and where a lot of them see it as a facility where boy meets girl and vice versa. Even in between lectures, on some of the campuses, during the time that they should be assimilating the lecture they have just had, and waiting for the next session from a different lecturer, they are grouping together and listening to music.

When you see such goings on, it makes you wonder - are they serious? And the impression is that they are not. Then you wonder; will they ever be? They are letting a golden opportunity roll by. There are some, I emphasise, routed pretty well; but even so, sometimes I find that having achieved the first objective they are not as enterprising as their foreign counterparts from within the Caribbean itself or even in west Africa. The ones out there need to be seen by the ones over here to see how well the ones out there are doing when it come to the faculties of learning. Those young people are always keen to go beyond the first hurdle and keep on rolling back the boundaries.

It is true; there are many of them out there in the Caribbean who have done pretty well.

They have actually excelled far more than the ones over here even though their beginning was far more humble than the ones here. Those children, from their earliest school days, would very often have had to walk much longer distances than the ones here simply to get a bus taking them miles away from their own communities; particularly if they had to go to secondary school. And they have not got the freedom of hopping on and hopping off a bus free-of-charge like their UK counterparts. Furthermore, in many cases, prior to getting to the class, they would have had more than their fair share of a tropical downpour which the ones over here probably never experience even right up to their adult life.

All this shows greater dedication; commitment; tenacity, and pride. These attributes are sadly lacking in the youngsters here. It is very glaring, the ones over here spending too much time on mobile phones, not being diverse or communicating with any other than their own little groups, entrenching each other into a negative way of thinking. Many of them would claim reading to be boring. Observing their actions, it is not difficult to see the lack of interest. Considering the beginning they have had, and the privilege that goes a-begging, they should be doing much more than simply reading sport or reading about celebrities and fashion. Their counterparts don't have time for such frivolity let alone the opportunity. Neither are they saturated with so much tripe from the negative tabloids.

That is why, when you are in the Caribbean and you meet groups of young people late in the evening - after their homework has been done - you find them talking about what they have learned at school and finding out how they are all progressing. This distributing of inspiration to each other and comparing with each other to elevate the standard; determined not to be left behind, draws a fascinating comparison with those brought up in Britain.

Yet I also blame many of the Caribbean adults over here who, by watching so much garbage on television, are presenting a very unbalanced view of the world to their children - to say the very least! These adults watch too many 'soaps' and far too few programmes that are more informative. In so doing, their kids get indoctrinated into an easy way of life instead of watching programmes that have a bearing on the present and the future. Then, when faced with more demanding challenges they rebel - they do not want to put in the effort required to master them. In some cases they go for sport or anything that is likely to exempt them from having to do too much thinking.

Yet even in sports, this trait of the African-Caribbean is very glaring. For example, most African-Caribbean athletes prefer sprinting. They will run the 100 and 200 metres; but that's it - they feel great. But long distance; they're not interested. It is also the case where not only endurance is required but also the thinking mind. A lot of them, a great many of them, do not enjoy going down that road because middle-distance to long-distance running requires an awareness which in turn entails exercising their brains. Not only that, but it also needs dedication to training. They only like what, in the main, comes easy; if it doesn't come natural, then they will not put in the work to become proficient in it.

And this is why, much as I am an admirer of sport, I am dismayed at the unbalanced attitude of African-Caribbean kids. I feel that, while sport is great, when you achieve success it should not be at the expense of education. Education has to be first and anything else has to be as a side show. If you are doing pretty well at it, you could stick to it, but not to the detriment of your educational development. Because, should you fail to achieve great heights in your chosen field of sport, you know definitely that you have a back-up of some consequence which could play a very fruitful role to your future and your future family.

However, if you take a typical African-Caribbean young man and ask him, what were the football results the previous night, he will most likely tell you accurately even if he does not support any of the victors or the vanquished. Yet ask him what was the headline story and - assuming it was not some trash celebrity, but something that has real bearing on day to day living by someone from the hierarchy, such as the prime minister explaining what the government is seeking to do to for the benefit of the nation - he might look at you, as if he had just seen the appearance of a ghost.

This is because most African-Caribbean young men, if and when they buy a newspaper, very seldom look at the front page. They go straight to the back page and then take it from there; probably the final three pages, where they can get sports results or see what the fixtures are going to be like. All this impacts on how they conduct their lives because, say they go for a job interview, well - they don't have the ability to approach it in the correct manner. You see; they lack flair because, to them, meeting someone else is an alien world to them. Now, had they been more proactive in reading the necessary materials it would have developed they mentality and supplemented their education. They would have learned more.

Another thing that strikes me badly is when I see kids that have just completed school at the age of 16 or 17 having to return to college classes simply to learn what they should have learnt four to five years earlier in main-stream school. This is a damning indictment on their state of development. Yet question them; when last did they read a book by simply going to the local library? It would be very disenchanting; their reply. You won't get any prize for guessing correctly. Asking them a simple question, which actually has a bearing on their existence; even if it is some proposal by the existing administration which is likely to be of benefit to them, they still probably won't be aware of it, because they are so detached. I would like parents, and the young people themselves, to know in this survey that proactive reading of various books is a wonderful bit of education in itself. And not simply on one particular ideal because this is a diverse world we have to remember.

By doing this it gives you some impetus for communicating with other people. That is, not just from your own group. It allows you to radiate that expression of contentment. Therefore when meeting others, it enables you to be more diverse and, by developing great self-confidence it helps you to learn from others through simple diverse communication. Yet, on the other hand, too much concentration of groups probably contributes to the vile attitude which seems to embrace our culture because, failing to diverse, it becomes difficult to extricate ourselves from the shackles of what like-minded people would embark upon. These people play to each other; they pride themselves as heroes; they like each other to see that they are dare-devils. They fail I see that there is a wider world apart from their own little groups.

Should they be able to cultivate a measure of pride, a reasonable amount of dignity, some self-esteem and the ability to cherish integrity, they would be appalled at the manner in which they currently choose to exist. To climb aboard the train of civility, you will have to jettison all of those negative ideals. Be confident, move away from it; that should be the order of the day. But as of now, these people are simply sick and I say it loud and clear - unambiguously. It is very easy within the fingers of one hand to see what the images are: too much belief in smoking a spliff; too much in the way of music with certain characters believing this is the height of life idolising a lot of so-call stars from other sections of the world, irrespective of the nature of the music - some of it good but some of it crass. Yet they fashion themselves to that, and enjoy the particular group, which is why we have so much unnecessary violence.

I do hope that the Mayor of London's mentoring scheme, which I have previously mentioned, will be embraced by our young men. Once implemented, they will, I'm sure, see this as a golden opportunity that should be cherished as a gift to them. One that would not probably have come from any other corner of the globe. Yet, on its own, this may not be enough. As I said earlier, the community at large should speak up and say to our young people, "Enough is enough - there is no place for this behaviour." But should they claim to be stereotyped; well, they are stereotyped by no one - but only by their own actions. It is there for all to see; if they do not wish to be stereotyped then I would suggest to them, "Move to the exit," because there they will see the light of redemption.

Should they feel aggrieved by the facts that are laid bare before them, they should be more aggrieved by their own unholy alliance. They should seek salvation and they would be embraced more readily by the more civilised communities, including African-Caribbean's. This would be more welcome. Those who seek riches by putting someone's well-being at risk are utterly low-minded; you cannot actually sink any lower. To move on to the heights, you have got to have a proper reappraisal of what is required. Then, once located, swing it into action and yourself pursue that course and it would improve your well-being, your life and that of your off-springs of tomorrow. For it means less dependence on the state, less incarceration and, by you seeking to get better recognition, you will become yourself a role model for following generations to come. But now, simply to be copying US convicts as role models and feeling that you are another man; well, for the time being, I would suggest that - wherein it is possible, given the abilities of the medical profession - you get a brain transplant.

Should I ever get the opportunity to meet Boris Johnson, the Mayor of London, I would like, on behalf of the African-Caribbean community, to express my thanks and gratitude for his wonderful initiative. I would also like to express thanks, through this medium, to all those who volunteer to contribute and assist such a hard-working community and salvage some pride for many of those African-Caribbean delinquents.

I hope that more mature adults do not shudder by this freshness of honesty; purity and truthfulness. It takes bravery in order to be so forthright. There is no more time for dilly-dallying, for time is moving by. If we want to be on the train of civilisation, our actions have to be our showcase. I am not condemning everyone with the same brush; I do have friends in the community and I am not enemies of the ones who I address so robustly, I simply want them to stop sleepwalking; look at themselves in great detail and swing it into action. Stop moaning and claiming a racist country or slavery; it is time to allow this, and the dust on it, to settle down.

If you want to move ahead, you should focus on the road ahead; clearly moving ahead or trying to, instead of only looking at years gone by. Otherwise it will not give much encouragement that you are actually charting a straight course. Rather it looks like you are going to run into a ditch or end up in something that you should not have come into contact with.

15 IN THE MIX

One of the beauties of the United Kingdom is that it is a cosmopolitan country. They have different groups; different cultures building into different enclaves. Within their own enclave some of the groups are hard-working and getting the due reward. Most of these groups have varied patterns of their own creation of economy. We have the Jews; a group within their own enclave who are renowned as business people; property owners; letting and occasionally sub-letting estate agents. They thrive at bakeries and newsagents and have their own clothes being manufactured by them. Seldom do they mix with the wider community. However, they do employ other groups where it is convenient for them to do so. In the main they seldom make the news in terms of disorder, fracas or violence; which is something to behold.

Beyond the Jews we have the Greeks. Their style of living is very much, in many respects, like the Jews. They probably have slightly wider boundaries and they do have more hairdressers and barbers' shops. Mainly being business people and property owners, they are seldom seen working on construction sites, which again is similar to the Jews. There are also Pakistanis and Bengalis; they are very much similar to each other in terms of lifestyle. Their communities thrive mainly on small shops and restaurants. Many of their shops are in close proximity to each other and duplicate one another. They live very much apart from anyone else. However, even though they live within the community, they tend - to some extent - to live outside the margin. When you get to know one or two they are inclined to be rather peaceful. However, one has to be careful how you socialise in any way with them. They are not like us in the West, where we like to be sociable and indulge in good natured banter. They can very easily be offended.

Now of all the groups that we have been considering, it is the Indians who top the list.

They are astute and highly resourceful; leading the field in small manufacturing workshops.

These workshops are predominantly within the textile industry. Yet even this group - through necessity - have entered the construction industry in a fairly big way. They have now reached the same level of skill and craft as the British-English and becoming very competitive, far in excess of the other ethnic groups. Their awareness and innovation have allowed them access into the skilled labour market beyond just carpentry and turned them into good plumbers and electricians. As their own population has expanded they are making highly valuable adaptations, not only to day-to-day living, by also enabling them to progress and prosper. The days when they ran textile businesses in the United Kingdom are fast becoming a thing of the past. They have also embarked into the import/export area and have branched out from beyond the boundaries of small corner shops and newsagents which have since been taken up by the Pakistanis and Bangladeshis. So no doubt the Indians are here for the long haul. They are very much carving their own niche market. They have moved into management, estate agents, architects, surveyors
and not least the medical profession.

Should any community feel that not sufficient is being done by the system and the establishment, though there are discrepancies, those groups ought to take a long hard look at their Indian neighbours. Try to understand them; analyse and assimilate, you will discover the virtues and wisdom that they possess. Within the Indian fraternity, there are many elements that the rest of us can derive great benefit from. We should study some of the Indian methods; observing how the youngsters, in their diligence and obedience to their elders, are prepared to assist within the business circle. The children also learn, while graduating from childhood to adolescent, to be competitive business people within their own rights. They are not prepared to take everything for granted. They systematically thrust forward to progress. Their desire to achieve economic success is a ceaseless quest. They make great sacrifices, forfeiting leisure time in their pursuit of education, technology and innovation; efficiency is embraced whole heartily by them.

They watch world events; they watch the pattern of events. If we take a little walk down in the heart of London as an example and - apart from the thriving surrounding areas on the outskirts of the city - pop into Tottenham

Court Road, you won't be long in noticing who the bosses are. All along this stretch of shops are modern electrical department stores stocking all the latest innovation of PC's; TVs; hand-sets; and any sort of radio; anything, in fact, of the modern era is sold. No doubt the Indians, on their own, hold a higher percentage of these shops than all the rest put together. Their work ethics are phenomenal. They are very business-like; constantly seeking to break new ground. There is not a great margin felt by them for members of any other group to compete.

And finally we come to African-Caribbean's. It is very difficult to identify what their positive traits actually are. I have mentioned in earlier paragraphs of the negatives but it is very hard to find the positives. Unfortunately those negative traits have been displayed all too graphically in recent times. I make no apologies for this description and for those mentioned earlier. Just think - many years ago, soon after entering the nuclear age, when we heard of Trident our mind would naturally go to nuclear weapons carried in water crafts and submarines; but now, if we only hear the tail-end of the news and we hear the word "Trident" - we are not so sure of what the newscaster had been referring to!

This is not a case of stereotyping - it is a fact of life and death. When we look at statistics, again without mentioning any group, and I ask everyone to tug at their heart and conscience - making it a private answer to their own self - when in London, you hear of a teen-age fatality from the hands of assailants; who are the ones that you would believe, initially, were the victims? Don't give me the answer; answer to your secret self. Then, you will begin to understand my point-of-view assuming you had not previously come to such an equation. So hence, I once again ask everyone concerned; everyone who desires to see a good notice written or good word spoken, to play their part to turn the tide.

In this respect, I take my hat off to the Mayor of London, Mr Boris Johnson, for the wonderful initiative where he has singled out black boys for special attention in an educational project and by recruiting seven thousand volunteers to assist in this £1.3M plan. The ball is now in the court of our African-Caribbean young men to show their mettle. Not to allow it to be all wasted. If they want to be recognised, as any of the other law-abiding groups, what a better challenge to justify the mayor's educational hand-out. It would indeed be nice to see some good come out of this. Hopefully make them stop and analyse their own attitudes and behaviour. But sometimes their desire for change, and longing to be a better part of civilisation, fails them.

Their current course has for a long time been a source of concern and utter dismay. It would be wonderful to show the public in general and the government in particular that they are becoming reformed characters. To achieve what is being asked of them would not go unnoticed in the eyes of the country. That the eyes of the country are focused on them could - up to a point - be seen as stereotyping. Yet this is only by their own actions. Lots are currently incarcerated. Now is the time to show that they can become decent citizens in their own right; carry themselves in a very dignified manner and I hope someday some of them, in whatever medium they happen to be, will reflect back and see what a much better position they have grafted themselves to be in - and in their hearts thank Mr Johnson for this tremendous work.

However the fact that he has taken time and invested so much to a particular group demonstrates that it was something of great necessity. Yet why though is it that within the 21st Century certain people of influence within the British system have suggested that the school-leaving age should be dropped to fourteen? Why, for so many decades, have we constantly had education kicked about in such a glare of publicity? Why can't we have a settled system? We are very aware that, as time goes on, changes are to be made; but why such frequent changes? Does it inspire confidence in the system for the under-16s? What do we think of previous education ministers? Were they or were they not doing a good job? Any business that had to be altered on such a regular basis would not inspire confidence.

So it is little wonder that we fail so many youngsters who leave school not ready to enter the work place. Maybe there is a case for not so many subjects to be taught to too many kids. Better that each child is evaluated to see where their strengths and weaknesses are. Then, when you see where their potential lay, you could educate them accordingly because, while we try to get lots of people into university, we also know - in our heart of hearts - that a lot of those people are not capable of being elevated to certain standards in certain fields of learning. So it is wasting their time and the time of the system; thus making it totally non-productive.

Therefore, it is about time that we in this country enjoyed a settled system of school education. It has been a mighty long time since we were supposed to have had academics, like those who went to Eton, Cambridge, and other leading universities, coming up with a credible and long lasting scheme where administrators of the classes do not have to keep having to alter their concepts of tuition. With a settled formula, which would not need to be reviewed for many years, those that have to administer students and pupils will be inspired with greater confidence and motivation in their vital calling.

16 PASSENGERS ON THE PLANET

So we can see why people within influential circles have, for many a day, been seeking to find a solution to the African-Caribbean youngsters' enigma. We have too often, in the recent past, heard them claiming that they are the way they are due to a lack of role models. Well, it would be nice if some of them decide to pioneer that special trait. At least they would feel they have achieved something which actually is a delight not only to themselves but to the community at large.

They have to make certain that the type of news and publicity which they create in the future will consign this current episode to the garbage of history. It should not be prolonged beyond now. Do not think of changing from tomorrow. So urgent is it; that it has got to be immediate - with sustained effort. Forget about trying to demonstrate yourselves as heroes to your mates. Be true to yourself. Seek true honour and you will enjoy the glory.

Because we, as passengers of this planet, see ourselves as possessing a wealth of knowledge, forgetting that the life expectancy - irrespective of whether you live to be a hundred and ten - is still a short time compared to the existence of the universe. None of us should believe that we can conquer, or be the master of the universe; it is a nigh-on impossibility, even though modern science has assisted our existence to a hitherto unknown degree. Yet, while we may bask in such exaltation, and privately being right to so cherish this moment of existence, could we have been able to so without technology? We may well have been laid to rest by now. However, not all is as it seems. We are in turmoil. How are people, who are just about pensionable age, going to cope with the demands and pressures of future days? All the influential people in our midst are moving around, hopping along on each others' backs like trapped ferrets witnessing the menacing approach of some four legged friend. What about the challenges that will face us in future days, when we have not been able to solve the immediate challenges? So while we bask in the glory of new discoveries, which benefit us to a large extent, the future problems are remorselessly piling on.

So, before we can think about solving future problems; try and get satisfaction by solving existing ones. For instance; how are we going to cope with people moving into the pension bracket? We are now making our own creation without the following or beyond. Many of the countries, who in past have scaled the heights; now find it difficult to find the answers to difficult questions. Our austerity in Britain is not temporary, it is prolonged. These are not prophecies designed for scaring, it is really to tug at the brain and give people a real awakening.

Influential people representing the state do not appear prepared to talk or discuss this because perhaps they may be finding this so perilous. They will probably delegate this to their successors while they themselves will be on the sidelines, probably rubbing their hands in glee that they will be not the ones to shoulder the demise of future days. Neither would they volunteer to answer those questions as to be beyond their limits. The cuts that have been requested, from so many governments in various parts of the world, are of utter savagery. I want the people of this country to think again and ask the right questions to their political masters. Should anyone elect to provide answers within the range; I beg of you to peer deeply into their eyes and search for the signs of nervousness.

We have climbed down a few notches in our standard of living. I ask the question of the British people, "Do you really believe there will be growth in the economy at some future date? And for some of you who have lost your homes or have had broken families or lost your businesses; do you genuinely believe you will in future recoup those loses?" Be honest with your own self and give your own self the reply.

Now, a lot of politicians who are in power in Britain, Europe and elsewhere - they know within themselves, but probably not wanting to reveal it publicly, that the standard to which their country of residence has dropped is too low. They will not, however, allow it to come back to the former glory days. So those whose livelihood has been decimated will also find it difficult to return to their winning ways. I am afraid it has gone forever. Much too much power is concentrated in too many of too few corners.

In Britain, I suspect, there is an eagerness by the existing administration to curb the power of the unions. I am not too sure to what effect that pursuit would happen; but whichever way - it is going to happen. The unions are on a slippery slope. Many members of the British people would like some relief from the prevailing plight yet they simply cannot afford to be on strike. One can sense, peering into the dark future but with immediate responsibilities, that they have no recourse; no choice; simply to soldier-on begrudgingly.

And when the administration realise this they are going to club not with leather gloves, but iron fist; because they know the electorate and public have no room to manoeuvre. Hence, the wages - as we once knew them - will be lagging behind in many sectors and therefore lower than the rate of inflation. This is because, with the influx of people from the EU, there is a pool of cheap labour. The private sector gives precedence to these workers at the expense of their British compatriots in their quest to increase profit margins. And they do this with no regard to their British counterparts who, for all they care, may perish in their attempts to make a living.

So why should our politicians try to soothe the anxieties of the British people by claiming that they are placing a cap on "Non-EU's?" We know that, even if they were to stop Non-EU's completely, we will still be sunk by migrants as long as there is wanton poverty ravaging mainland Europe. We are waiting; by 2030 a new wave of migrants will be eligible to come here. That is from countries newly joined to the EU. And also from the regions that span the divide between Europe and Asia. How do we know how many will arrive when they finally enter. Predicting what the population growth will be in 2030 is like pulling rabbits out of a magician's hat. But by then we would have run out of space.

Well, if anyone wants to have a measure as to the underlying poverty in Britain, and hardship; which is very close to poverty, they have only to drive on the main roads of the capital.

The sheer volume of shops along the way - duplicating each other - this is a reasonable yardstick to use. If you are an activist of any consequence, one would be seriously asking questions of all concerned, "How do your businesses stay in existence?" It might beggar belief to reveal the knowledge of seeing supposedly fit young men scavenging on the streets of Britain. In particular, in the huge rubbish bins outside some of the bakers where you see them foraging for loaves that have been discarded. Coming, even, with their own ready bags - in pairs - as if on a shopping venture. Yet why is it necessary for them to eke out such an existence? Is it by virtue of the tough going that they are forced to do anything for survival?

Perhaps, with the influx of skilled workers from abroad, it is because we now have an abundance of handy-men. If this paradigm is understood then it is beginning to shed light to the reader why it impacts on British skilled workers. Because in order to enter the labour market, reminding you of the dire needs of those individuals, we are faced with foreign workers who can enter at a much cheaper rate than what the British are used to. However, with the prevailing austerity measures that most of Western Europe is experiencing, it is little wonder why citizens of the United Kingdom are prepared to embrace that extravagantly rich source of cheap labour.

Consequently there are some migrant workers who earn a decent living by having to make such temporary adjustment and sacrifices to fulfil their ambitions. Yet, because a lot of them are sharing flats and splitting the rent they are making great savings. Not only that but, with all that body-heat, they're not even having to fork out on heating bills! Now, when we talk about growth - we are also talking about recovery. But in these days of internet communication, wherever they are - within the member states - they acquire the same knowledge of recovery as we have. So the Achilles heel of "Freedom of Movement" ensures that migrants - who may have left when the going got tough - flood back through our "Open Door" policy to share the spoils.

But what about millions of pounds that government has put into training young people to acquire skills? You can see how it is so easily negated because, by virtue of the European Treaty, we are building a vast source of cheap labour. So because our nation hopes to enjoy cheaper labour than what it should have otherwise have been, our youngsters will be forever squabbling for cheap jobs which are not really worth their while.

Now whilst people will say, "The Europeans are working cheaply, why can't we?" there is a very black hole that exists, whatever you may do, until you get rid of that European treaty. Because how can you charge an individual fairly for work wanted to be carried out? Once you take into account the tax taken by the Inland Revenue, that job will become out of reach. So you cannot compete - even if you wanted to - with migrant workers. Also, you are not able to employ staff for less take-home pay the way they do. So you have to ask the prospective clients a higher sum and this is where your effort strikes the buffers. You are therefore deemed to be too expensive.

Back in the final decade of the 20th Century, from 1990 to the year 2000 the British carpenter and the British bricklayer would have commanded £140 - £150 a day. But in the first decade of the 21st Century they could not get anywhere near that for a day's work. Going back to 1990 we have also seen how prices have risen considerably. The Council Tax in itself has risen by an enormous extent. All the utility bills have gone up many folds; be it electricity supply, gas, water rates or telephone bills - it has all gone up by leaps and bounds. Now, a decade into the 21st Century, our wages have actually declined. The wages of the skilled British worker has gone down. So how does he exist with such a yawning gap? He is certainly a strong candidate for the arms of poverty.

But could this result in adopting what is called Social Cleansing? That is, wanting to move people from certain areas. If so it will be a frightening harbinger of worse to come.

Because, once adopted, such sinister policies will widen to include ever more victims. Then the pressure will be building. And we shall be creating more criminal elements. This will be out of frustration because if you keep pushing the people who are 'have-nots', and grouping them into certain areas, you will be creating 'No-Go' areas.

Therefore you will be finding the results, a few years later, on the streets. In this respect, it will have a back-lash. In those sorts of areas you will never have your own culture. Which means, in effect, that you will be promoting the very evil you have been fighting to avoid. So, in trying to fill up one particular hole, you are creating others. And as long as people can see such a vast divide you will not win their hearts and minds. No matter how much you preach, it doesn't matter. Because there will be kids growing up, whole families in fact, that will be living on the bread line.

Well, influential people - when they read these passages - might want to come and pour scorn simply because it does not emanate from them; but from an ordinary mortal. So what? I have no qualms; common-sense and imagination are not the domain of any particular sector. We have fortitude as our own right and if the people, who we look upon to be our guides, are not always correct then there are many such moments in life when you have to look at the reasoning very objectively. The yardstick of history can sometimes be highly influential as a template for both present and future.

The egos of those who believe they are super-human by virtue of an educational background appear to forget we are dealing with the planet earth and none of them are masters of the universe. We all have to be subservient to its whims. We have to give way to its call at any given time. We cannot take it for granted; it has to be respected and we need to be grateful to what is on offer. Looking at the different states of the world, various nations, space at the top is only for the lucky few - not for the great many who aspire to that summit. Many of those who have been at the summit are now on a journey that will be regarded as the slippery slope. And we the people are, I am afraid, in increasingly vast numbers going to have to adjust permanently.

17 THANK YOU

Thank you for purchasing my book, it was a labour of love and I truly hope you enjoyed reading it.

I'm Winston Payne.

ABOUT THE AUTHOR

Author Winston Payne, a West Indian immigrant from St. Lucia, found himself on the shores of the British Isles back in the early 1960's.

Winston Payne like his father, who he left back in St. Lucia, had a rosy coloured view of the country, but what he found on his arrival was very different. He shares with you his experiences through the years, how his love for his new home begins to grow and how his experiences in education, gave him another perspective. How the countries current leap into opening the door to Eastern European migrants has started to change the look and feel of Britain. For the good? Reading what this book has to say will reveal a surprising answer.

He recalls the early days of work, racism and his love of boxing. Winston gives a balanced view not only of his life in the early days, but the hard years which followed, all the way through to the present.

For more than 5 decades he's seen Britain change, bend, and buckle under social and economic times. Giving a fresh, balanced and many would say, truthful description of how Britain is coping with social injustice and the political landscape both in the UK and Europe.

www.ingramcontent.com/pod-product-compliance
Lightning Source LLC
Chambersburg PA
CBHW070548290526
45790CB00002B/604